Dedicated to Father John Schwantes,
a Jesuit Pope Francis would be proud of.

—Michael V. Uschan

Other books in the People in the News series:

Adele
Halle Berry
Beyoncé
Justin Bieber
Sandra Bullock
James Cameron
Fidel Castro
Hillary Clinton
George Clooney
Stephen Colbert
Suzanne Collins
Natalie Coughlin
Ellen Degeneres
Johnny Depp
Eminem
Roger Federer
50 Cent
James Franco
Glee Cast and Creators
Selena Gomez
Ryan Gosling
Jeff Gordon
Neil Patrick Harris
Anne Hathaway
Salma Hayek
Jennifer Hudson
Jay-Z
Wyclef Jean
Angelina Jolie
Alicia Keys
Taylor Lautner
Spike Lee
Jet Li
George Lopez
Jennifer Lopez

Jane Lynch
Eli Manning
Stephenie Meyer
Nicki Minaj
Walter Dean Myers
Barack Obama
Michelle Obama
Apolo Anton Ohno
Jamie Oliver
Sarah Palin
Danica Patrick
Katy Perry
Tyler Perry
David Patraeus
Oscar Pistorius
Amy Poehler
Prince Harry
Muammar Qaddafi
Condoleezza Rice
Rihanna
Alex Rodriguez
Seth Rogen
Derrick Rose
J.K. Rowling
Shakira
Kelly Slater
Jon Stewart
Taylor Swift
Tim Tebow
Usher
Lindsey Vonn
Denzel Washington
Shaun White
Serena Williams
Mark Zuckerberg

Contents

Fame and celebrity are alluring. People are drawn to those who walk in fame's spotlight, whether they are known for great accomplishments or for notorious deeds. The lives of the famous pique public interest and attract attention, perhaps because their experiences seem in some ways so different from, yet in other ways so similar to, our own.

Newspapers, magazines, and television regularly capitalize on this fascination with celebrity by running profiles of famous people. For example, television programs such as *Entertainment Tonight* devote all their programming to stories about entertainment and entertainers. Magazines such as *People* fill their pages with stories of the private lives of famous people. Even newspapers, newsmagazines, and television news frequently delve into the lives of well-known personalities. Despite the number of articles and programs, few provide more than a superficial glimpse at their subjects.

Lucent's People in the News series offers young readers a deeper look into the lives of today's newsmakers, the influences that have shaped them, and the impact they have had in their fields of endeavor and on other people's lives. The subjects of the series hail from many disciplines and walks of life. They include authors, musicians, athletes, political leaders, entertainers, entrepreneurs, and others who have made a mark on modern life and who, in many cases, will continue to do so for years to come.

These biographies are more than factual chronicles. Each book emphasizes the contributions, accomplishments, or deeds that have brought fame or notoriety to the individual and shows how that person has influenced modern life. Authors portray their subjects in a realistic, unsentimental light. For example, Bill Gates—cofounder of the software giant Microsoft—has been instrumental in making personal computers the most vital tool of the modern age. Few dispute his business savvy, his perseverance, or his technical expertise, yet critics say he is ruthless in his dealings with competitors and driven more by his desire to maintain Microsoft's dominance in the computer industry than by an interest in furthering technology.

In these books, young readers will encounter inspiring stories about real people who achieved success despite enormous obstacles. Oprah Winfrey—one of the most powerful, most watched, and wealthiest women in television history—spent the first six years of her life in the care of her grandparents while her unwed mother sought work and a better life elsewhere. Her adolescence was colored by pregnancy at age fourteen, rape, and sexual abuse.

Each author documents and supports his or her work with an array of primary and secondary source quotations taken from diaries, letters, speeches, and interviews. All quotes are footnoted to show readers exactly how and where biographers derive their information and provide guidance for further research. The quotations enliven the text by giving readers eyewitness views of the life and accomplishments of each person covered in the People in the News series.

In addition, each book in the series includes photographs, annotated bibliographies, timelines, and comprehensive indexes. For both the casual reader and the student researcher, the People in the News series offers insight into the lives of today's newsmakers—people who shape the way we live, work, and play in the modern age.

The Surprise Pope

In the hundreds of millions of words that have been written and spoken about Argentine Cardinal Jorge Mario Bergoglio since he was elected Pope Francis on March 13, 2013, perhaps no word has been used more often than "surprise." In its story about his selection, the German newspaper *Der Spiegel* (*The Mirror*) labeled him "The Surprise Pope," as did many other print and online publications. The choice of the seventy-six-year-old Bergoglio was surprising because he was so little known and because he was from South America. But his selection to head the world's 1.2 billion Roman Catholics was only the first of many surprises the new pope had for the world.

The new pope traditionally makes his first public appearance on a balcony of Saint (St.) Peter's Basilica that overlooks St. Peter's Square in Rome, Italy. Despite rain, over one hundred thousand people had gathered in the square to see the new pope. About seventy minutes after his fellow cardinals had elevated Bergoglio to their church's highest office, Cardinal Jean-Louis Tauran of France stepped onto the balcony and spoke the traditional Latin phrase "*Habemus Papam!*" which means, "We have a pope!"[1] Tauran then announced Bergoglio's name as well as the new name he had taken as pope.

Bergoglio's name was met with silence from the gathered crowd because many people had never heard of him. His selection even stunned people knowledgeable about the church and which cardinal might be elected. Father Adriano Furgoni, a Catholic priest from Rome waiting in the square, admitted he was amazed Bergoglio had been chosen, saying in shock, "I didn't expect it, I didn't expect it."[2] Neither did many other people.

Despite confusion over who the new pope was, thousands of people cheered when Francis appeared. He greeted them with "*Buona sera,*" Italian for "Good evening," and jokingly told them, "You know, it's the duty of the cardinals to find a new pope. Well, it seems that they went almost to the end of the world to find him, but here we are."[3] His humorous comment was greeted with laughter. Cardinal Bergoglio had been archbishop of Buenos Aires, Argentina, which is 6,934 miles (11,160km) from Rome and located at the bottom of South America.

Pope Francis I smiles as a lamb is placed around his neck during a visit to a living nativity scene in a town outside Rome, Italy, in January 2014. Symbolically the pope is considered the shepherd of the Catholic Church.

Occasional shouts of "*Il Papa*" and "*Francesco,*" Italian for "pope" and "Francis," erupted from a few people as the pope talked. Before giving a papal blessing to end his appearance, Francis made a request that once again silenced the gigantic crowd. In a show of humility that astonished the thousands gathered in the square, Francis asked them to pray for him before he blessed them. Francis later made the same request of people around the world by tweeting, "Please pray for me."[4] When Francis ended several moments of silence by blessing people below him, they joyously began chanting over and over "*Viva il Papa,*" Italian for "Long live the pope."

The surprise the faithful in St. Peter's Square felt when they learned the name of the new pope was shared by millions of people around the world. That emotion was heightened by several historic factors connected with his selection.

Francis Makes History

Bergoglio's election was historic and surprising in several ways, including the fact that his predecessor—Pope Benedict XVI—still lived. The eighty-six-year-old Benedict had resigned as pope on February 28, 2013, citing age as the reason why he was no longer capable of fulfilling the duties of his office. Benedict, who had headed the church since 2005, was the first pope to resign since Pope Gregory XII in 1415. Thus, whoever was elected his successor would face the difficult task of being pope while another pope still lived, a situation that could lead to questions of which pope was in charge. Luckily, Benedict has not questioned anything Francis has done.

The church's 266th pope also made history by being the first from South America. A South American pope made sense because that continent is home to 42 percent of the world's Catholics. However, it still surprised people because only Europeans had been elected pope for nearly 1,300 years. The last non-European pope was Gregory III, who was born in Syria and ruled for a ten-year period ending in 741. Francis is also the first pope who is a Jesuit, or a member of the Society of Jesus, the order of priests founded in 1534 by Ignatius of Loyola, who was elevated to sainthood by the Catholic Church in 1622. Francis is the first pope from a religious order since Gregory XVI in 1831, who was a monk in the Camaldolese order.

The papal name Bergoglio chose was also historic and surprising because most popes have taken the names of notable popes from the past. Twenty-one popes have been named John, sixteen Gregory or Benedict, and fourteen Clement. The new pope reveals his name to his fellow cardinals in a traditional ceremony after they have elected him. When Bergoglio was asked what name he had chosen, he amazed the cardinals by answering that he would be the first pope named Francis. The cardinals immediately knew Bergoglio had chosen that name to honor St. Francis of Assisi, who in 1209 founded the order of priests known as Franciscans and is one of the church's most revered saints.

Several days later in a news conference, Francis explained why he had chosen his new name. Francis said he was becoming nervous as it became apparent he would be chosen to head the Catholic Church. Seeing his distress, Cardinal Cláudio Hummes of São Paulo, Brazil, a good friend, talked to him to comfort him. When Bergoglio was elected, Hummes gave him the inspiration for his papal name. "[Hummes] hugged me, he kissed me and he said 'don't forget the poor.' That word, the poor, lodged in me here [Francis tapped his head]. It was then that I thought of St Francis. And then I thought of wars and about peace and that's how the name came to me—a man of peace, a poor man . . . and how I would like a church of the poor, for the poor."[5]

St. Francis had devoted his life to helping the poor, who in his era were often neglected by the church. Bergoglio was also known for his humility, his simple lifestyle, and his desire to bring the word of God to everyone. In the days and months after Bergoglio became pope, people around the world began to realize the new pope had chosen the right name because his words and actions so clearly matched the spirit of St. Francis who had lived nine centuries earlier.

Chapter 1

A Humble Beginning

Francis is the 266th pope in a line of succession dating back to the year A.D. 33 when St. Peter became head of the Catholic Church after Jesus Christ died by crucifixion. The vast majority of popes—216 of them—have been Italian, and Francis could almost be considered the 217th because of his family heritage. Although Jorge Mario Bergoglio was born in Buenos Aires, Argentina, his father, Mario, was born in Italy. His mother, Regina María Sivori, was born in Argentina but her mother had emigrated from Italy and her father was of Italian ancestry.

Mario and his parents, Giovanni Angelo Bergoglio and Rosa Margarita Vasallo Bergoglio, moved from Italy to Argentina in 1929 because they feared their homeland's future under dictator Benito Mussolini. When Mussolini came to power in 1922, he began taking civil liberties away from citizens and ruthlessly ruled Italy in a style of government known as fascism. María Elena Bergoglio, the pope's only surviving sibling, says, "I remember that my father repeated often that the advent of fascism was the reason that really pushed him to leave."[6] Another factor that may have hastened the family's departure from Italy was the brave way Rosa had publicly spoken against Mussolini's tyranny. María Elena said, "Grandmother Rosa was a heroine for us, a very brave lady. I'll never forget when she told us how in her town, in Italy, she took the pulpit to condemn the dictatorship, Mussolini, fascism."[7]

The Bergoglios chose Argentina as their new home because three of Mario's brothers had moved there in 1922. That decision was the first step in a chain of events that resulted in the first pope from South America.

A Future Pope Is Born

Twenty-one-year-old Mario and his parents arrived in Buenos Aires from Genoa, Italy, on January 25, 1929, after a voyage of several months aboard the ocean liner *Giulio Cesare* (Julius Caesar). Even though the day was very hot and humid, Rosa set foot on Argentine soil for the first time wearing a heavy coat with a fur collar. She wore it because money from the sale of the family business and other possessions in Italy was concealed in its lining.

The family lived in a large four-story building the Bergoglio brothers had built in Flores, a large middle-class barrio (neighborhood) in Buenos Aires. The building, which also housed their successful flooring company, was the first in Buenos Aires to have an elevator and is still standing today. In 1932, however, the business failed due to an economic crisis that devastated Argentina and left the entire family with almost no money.

Jorge Mario Bergoglio, the future Pope Francis, is seen in an undated photo from his youth in Argentina.

A Fateful Voyage

Mario Bergoglio and his parents were among 535,000 Italians who moved to Argentina in the decade of the 1920s. The Bergoglio family arrived in Buenos Aires on January 25, 1929, aboard the ocean liner *Giulio Cesare* (Julius Caesar). The family originally had purchased tickets to sail from Genoa, Italy, to Argentina on the *Principessa* [Princess] *Mafalda* almost two years earlier. However, their move to Argentina was delayed while they finished selling their property. When the ship was built in 1908, the *Mafalda* had been the largest passenger liner in the world, but by 1927, though still considered luxurious, it was badly in need of repairs. The delay was a stroke of good fortune for the Bergoglios. The *Mafalda* sank off the coast of Brazil on October 25, 1927, when a propeller fractured and damaged the hull and 314 of its 1,252 passengers died. Pope Francis has acknowledged how lucky his family was that it never boarded the *Mafalda*: "They disembarked from the 'Julius Caesar,' though they should have sailed on an earlier voyage: with the 'Princess Mafalda,' which sank. You cannot imagine how many times I have thanked divine Providence!"

Jorge Mario Bergoglio. "The Story of a Vocation." *L'Osservatore Romano*, January 3, 2014. http://vaticanresources.s3.amazonaws.com/pdf%2FING_2014_001_0301.pdf.

In Italy, Mario had known many priests from the Society of St. Francis de Sales, an order known as the Salesians. When Mario arrived in Buenos Aires, he became friends with Salesian Father Enrique Pozzoli. The priest helped arrange a loan so Mario's parents could buy a store in Flores after the family flooring business had collapsed. Mario, who had been an accountant in Italy, did the bookkeeping for the store and made deliveries. Two years later, Mario met Regina during mass at San Antonio Chapel and they were married on December 12, 1935.

Mario and Regina Bergoglio bought a home in Flores to be close to both their families. On December 17, 1936, Jorge Mario was born. Pozzoli baptized the newborn infant on Christmas Day in the Basilica of San Carlos Borromeo; Pozzoli would continue to play an important role in the life of the future pope. The Bergoglios had four more children—sons Alberto Horacio and Oscar Adrian and daughters Marta Regina and María Elena.

A Happy Childhood

Jorge's grandmother, Rosa, began babysitting Jorge because Alberto was only thirteen months younger than Jorge and it was difficult for their mother to care for two infants at the same time. Living nearby, she would pick him up in the morning and return him home at night. As a result, Jorge became very close to his grandmother, whom he lovingly called "*nonna*," Italian for "grandmother." She spent hours telling him stories about Italy. Although his father only spoke Spanish to Jorge because he wanted him to be fluent in the language of his new homeland, Rosa taught Jorge how to speak Piedmontese, an Italian dialect spoken by people in the Piedmont region in the northwest corner of Italy where the Bergoglios had lived.

Rosa influenced Jorge in many ways. One of the most important things she did was to introduce him to basic Catholic religious beliefs. She taught him his first prayers and was his godmother when he was baptized. The pope has said, "The one who had the greatest impact on me was my grandmother, who taught me the faith and read me the lives of the saints."[8] His parents were also religious and helped Jorge strengthen his belief in God. In addition to regularly attending mass at the Basilica San José de Flores, the family participated in festivals and processions that honored saints or key religious events. As an altar boy at San José, Jorge helped priests by carrying a cross, candle, or the Bible onto the altar when mass began and performing other minor duties during mass. He performed those duties early in the morning before school started.

Jorge was an active boy who had a passion for sports. He played basketball like his father but his favorite sport was soccer.

Elsa Scigliano, a childhood friend, remembers that the future pope got into trouble once while playing soccer with neighborhood friends. Scigliano said, "He played in the street. One time, playing football [soccer], he broke a window of a neighbor's house [with the ball]. He went to say he was sorry. He always apologized."[9] Jorge became a loyal fan of the local San Lorenzo de Almagro soccer team, a passion he still had when elected pope.

The Bergoglios were a happy family and did many things together. They played games including the Spanish card game *brisca*. On Saturdays the children would listen to the opera on the radio with their mother, who would explain the stories and music. As an adult, the pope admitted he sometimes fell asleep during the performances. But he also said those happy times with his mother and siblings helped him develop a love of fine music. And every Sunday after church, the family and other relatives would gather at the Bergoglio home and enjoy a huge lunch with up to a half-dozen courses of food.

Young Jorge Mario Bergoglio is on the second row from the top and sixth from the left in this undated group photo from his primary school in Buenos Aires, Argentina.

Jorge attended San Juan Bosco, a Catholic elementary school where his teachers were Salesian nuns. Jorge grew to love the nuns; decades later when he became Archbishop of Buenos Aires, he celebrated mass annually at the school. When Jorge was thirteen and ready to enter high school, his father had a surprise for him—he had to go to work while continuing his education at Antonio Cervino High School!

Learning the Value of Work

His father's decision shocked Jorge. Although the Bergoglios were not rich—they had no car and did not travel on vacations—his father earned enough money as an accountant working for several firms so that they had a decent life. But Mario wanted his son to learn the value of hard work at an early age, so he got him a job in a hosiery factory for which he did accounting. Jorge worked there as a cleaner for two years and in his third year was promoted to clerical and administrative work. His work shift was after school from 2 P.M. to 8 P.M.

In his fourth year of high school, Jorge switched to the Escuela Nacional de Educación Técnica, a technical school, and began studying chemistry. He also continued working, taking a job in a chemical factory from 7 A.M. to 1 P.M. to further his goal of becoming a chemist. After an hour break for lunch, Jorge would attend classes until 8 P.M. It was a demanding schedule for a teenager. But in a book published in 2010, Bergoglio admitted the experience taught him how important it was for people to have a job: "Neither inheritance, family upbringing, nor education bestow the anointing of dignity. It only comes through work [and] if we do not work, dignity crumbles."[10]

It was while working in the chemical laboratory that Esther Balestrino de Careaga, his boss, taught Jorge another lesson about work—that he had to do every task as completely and as well as he could. Jorge once handed in a chemical analysis she had requested. When de Careaga was surprised he had finished it so quickly, she asked him if he had actually done the test. Jorge answered that he had not because it was a routine test. "I would answer, 'What for?' If I'd done all the previous tests, it would be

Jorge Learns to Cook

One of the most interesting books about Pope Francis is *Pope Francis: Conversations with Jorge Bergoglio*. When it was first printed in 2010, while Francis was still a cardinal, it was titled simply *El Jesuita*, Spanish for *The Jesuit*. The book consists mainly of conversations authors Sergio Rubin and Francesca Ambrogetti had with Bergoglio on many topics. His answers provide interesting insights into his personality and life. The birth of his sister María Elena Bergoglio when he was twelve temporarily weakened his mother so much that she had trouble cooking for her husband and five children. In the book, Bergoglio explains how his mother taught him and his younger siblings to cook by giving them directions when they came home after school:

> My mother became paralyzed after giving birth to her fifth child, although she recovered over time. [When] we got home from school, we'd find her seated, peeling potatoes, with all the other ingredients laid out. Then she'd tell us how to mix and cook them, because we didn't have a clue. "Now put this in the pot and that in the pan . . . " she'd explain. That's how we learned to cook. We can all cook veal escalopes, at least.

Sergio Rubin and Francesca Ambrogetti. *Pope Francis: Conversations with Jorge Bergoglio.* New York: G. P. Putnam's Sons, 2013, p. 11.

more or less the same. 'No, you have to do things properly,' she would chide me. In short, she taught me the seriousness of hard work. Truly, I owe a huge amount to that great woman."[11]

Jorge still managed to have fun despite his busy schedule. Like teenagers around the world, one of the things he enjoyed the most was dancing. Jorge liked the tango, Argentina's national dance, as well as the milonga, a faster dance similar to the tango that was also popular then. Oscar Crespo, a teenage friend of Jorge's, remembers, "We used to go dancing at the clubs in the

Chacarita district [of Buenos Aires] because there were a lot of girls."[12] Crespo also said Jorge dated one of the girls from Chacarita.

But when Jorge was seventeen, something happened to him. The experience was so powerful that it ended his dancing and dating days and made him determined to become a priest.

A Call from God

Although the future pope's early years were unremarkable as he enjoyed activities other teenagers did such as sports and music, his grandmother and parents had instilled in him a deep belief in and love for his Catholic faith. Jorge displayed that religious fervor at age thirteen. When Jorge began high school, he asked all his classmates if they had celebrated their first communion, the act during mass of eating a thin wafer of unleavened bread that symbolically represents the body of Christ. When Jorge discovered that four students had not, he helped them learn about the sacred rite so they could start receiving communion. Alberto Omodei was one of those four students. After Bergoglio was elected pope, Omodei said, "He already had that vocation [to be a priest]. He had a desire to bring people closer to God."[13]

At one time or another, many little Catholic boys think about becoming a priest, usually because they believe it would make them special or powerful. Pope Francis admits that happened to him at a young age: "I felt my vocation for the first time . . . [during] the sixth grade, and I spoke about it with [a Salesian priest]. But then I began secondary school and 'goodbye!'"[14] The desire to be a priest quickly left him as he got caught up in new experiences in high school and began to dream instead about becoming a chemist. The joy Jorge had in dancing and socializing with his friends further pushed thoughts of becoming a priest out of his mind.

On September 21, 1954, Jorge was on his way to a train station to meet with a group of friends so they could travel into the countryside for a picnic. That day was "Día de la primavera," an Argentine holiday that celebrates the first day of spring in the southern hemisphere. It was also known as Student Day because high school and college students had the day off.

On the way to the train station, the seventeen-year-old stopped to pray at Basilica San José de Flores, the church he and his family attended. That decision changed his life when he met Father Carlos B. Duarte Ibarra. Even though he did not know the priest, Jorge decided to go to confession. In the Catholic Church, people confess their sins to a priest to seek forgiveness

from God. In a book written before he became pope, Francis described his encounter with Ibarra. "Something strange happened to me in that confession. I don't know what it was, but it changed my life. I think it surprised me, caught me with my guard down. [From] that moment on, for me, God is the One who *te primerea*—'springs it on you.' You search for Him, but He searches for you first. You want to find Him, but he finds you first."[15]

The powerful emotions he experienced made Jorge realize that God wanted him to become a priest, so Jorge went home instead of continuing on to meet his friends for a picnic. His sister María Elena explained that his decision not to join his friends was especially meaningful because of one of the young women in the group. In an interview after her brother became pope, she claimed her brother was going to ask the girl to marry him. She said, "On that spring day, September 21, he was supposed to propose to her," adding in a joking way, "But if I keep telling this story, my brother will end up excommunicating [ban from the Church] me."[16]

Even though Jorge knew in his heart that day that he wanted to become a priest, he did not immediately enter a seminary, a school that educates men to become priests. The teenager also kept his decision secret—he did not even tell his family—and he continued to study chemistry.

Seventeen-year-old Jorge Mario Bergoglio felt confirmation that God wanted him to become a priest at the Basilica San José de Flores in Buenos Aires, Argentina.

"Miserando Atque Eligendo"

Pope Francis has never forgotten that most important experience in his life. When priests become bishops, cardinals, or popes, they choose a motto for themselves that has deep personal meaning. The motto Francis chose when he became a bishop in 1992, and which he retained as archbishop, cardinal, and pope, reflects the importance of the change that took place within him on that spring day in 1954. It is *"Miserando atque eligendo,"* a Latin phrase that means "because he saw him through the eyes of mercy and chose him."

The saying is associated with a famous commentary on the Bible story in which Jesus asks Matthew, who as a tax collector was shunned by other people and considered a sinner, to become one of his disciples. For Francis, the phrase is an admission that he also felt unworthy that God had asked him to become a priest. A further reminder of that day is a personal statement Francis wrote on December 13, 1969, when he was ordained a priest. It includes these lines: "I believe in my history—which was pierced by God's look of love, on the first day of spring, Sept. 21—he came to meet me and invited me to follow him."[17] Francis even today carries that statement with him in his daily prayer book wherever he goes.

Chapter 2

A Jesuit Priest

Jorge Mario Bergoglio knew he was destined to become a priest after his life-altering experience on September 21, 1954. Realizing that priests are celibate (not allowed to marry), he ended his relationship with the young woman who was his tango partner and girlfriend. But Bergoglio did not immediately enter a seminary. Instead, his wide-ranging intellect led him to explore other subjects before beginning his studies to become a priest. "Let's say that God left the door open for me for a few years,"[18] is how Bergoglio described this period of his life.

In a period of intellectual inquisitiveness common to young people, Bergoglio became an avid reader of classic literature, including poetry by Italians Dante Alighieri and Alessandro Manzoni and German Johann Hölderlin. He enjoyed not only the artistry of their works but their intellectual messages. Bergoglio also became intensely interested in politics, especially how governments could alleviate widespread poverty in Argentina and other South American countries.

Many South Americans in the 1950s began to believe a Communist government would ease their poverty. Bergoglio has admitted that part of his political education included reading Communist publications. However, Bergoglio rejected communism as a solution to poverty. Although communism attempts to treat all people equally economically, it is a totalitarian form of government that reduces personal freedom and denies people a say in how their government operates. Enrique Gallini, a co-worker at the chemical lab where Bergoglio continued to work, remembers that Bergoglio would argue passionately with fellow lab employees who were Communists about their political philosophy. But even while watching Bergoglio engage in such heated debates, Gallini claims he knew his friend's future was as a priest: "I wasn't surprised at his vocation. The Catholic Church, and its way of thinking, was already in his heart. He was always very humble."[19]

Most people, however, had no inkling Bergoglio wanted to become a priest because he continued to study chemistry and worked several jobs including one as a nightclub bouncer. Bergoglio was even able to keep his secret from his parents for nearly a year until one day when his mother was cleaning his room.

Help from Father Pozzoli

Regina Bergoglio was puzzled when she found theology books in Jorge's room. Regina had assumed they were medical texts because Bergoglio had told her he was studying medicine as well

Bergoglio (center) is photographed with schoolmates outside his preparatory school. His parents encouraged him to finish college before making up his mind about the priesthood.

as chemistry. The discovery led her to call her son to the room to explain the religious books: "Jorge! Come here! Didn't you tell me you were going to study medicine?" "Yes, Mama," he answered. "Why do you lie to me?" she asked, pointing to the theology books. "I am not lying to you, Mama," Jorge replied. "I am going to study the medicine of the soul."[20]

When Bergoglio's parents learned of his decision in November 1955, they were not sure if they wanted their eighteen-year-old son to become a priest because they feared his life would be one of self-sacrifice, hardship, and loneliness. They told him to finish college and then decide. Their negative response led Bergoglio to talk to Enrique Pozzoli, the Salesian priest who was still a close family friend. Bergoglio told Pozzoli of his priestly vocation and asked his help in convincing his parents that the decision was a good one.

On December 12, 1955, Mario and Regina Bergoglio celebrated their twentieth wedding anniversary with morning mass at the Basilica of San José de Flores. Pozzoli conducted mass, and the Bergoglios invited him to breakfast. During the meal, Pozzoli began talking about how he decided to become a priest and how others had made that life-altering decision. Bergoglio was amazed at how skillfully Pozzoli eased his parents into the discussion of Bergoglio's desire to become a priest without trying to force them to accept his decision, although they did not necessarily like it. In a letter Bergoglio wrote decades later, he said Pozzoli was key in helping his parents accept his decision: "Well, at this point 'finally' my parents' hearts had melted. . . . Then the decision came on its own, freely from those with whom he was speaking. They didn't feel forced . . . but he had prepared their hearts. He had sown, and well . . . but he left the enjoyment of the harvest to others."[21]

Bergoglio quit his studies in chemistry in 1956 and entered the Inmaculada Concepción Seminary in Buenos Aires. The Inmaculada Seminary trained priests for the Archdiocese of Buenos Aires, a territorial unit of the Catholic Church that today encompasses 78 square miles (200 sq. km) and has 183 parishes serving nearly 2.7 million Catholics. His path to becoming a priest, however, would soon take an unexpected and painful turn.

The Bergoglio family appears in an undated photograph. Standing (left to right) are brother Alberto Horacio, Jorge Mario, Oscar Adrian, and sister Marta Regina. Sitting are sister María Elena, mother Regina María Sivori, and father Mario Jose Francisco.

Bergoglio Becomes a Jesuit

In August 1957, Bergoglio became severely ill with pneumonia. Three cysts formed on tissue in his right lung, and doctors had to remove the upper part of the lung. Bergoglio was on the brink

Bergoglio Fails Father Pozzoli

Salesian priest Enrique Pozzoli played an important role in the life of Jorge Mario Bergoglio by baptizing the future pope and helping reconcile his parents to his decision to become a priest. But in a letter Bergoglio once wrote praising Pozzoli, he admitted that he failed to console Pozzoli when he was dying. Bergoglio, then a twenty-five-year-old seminarian, went to visit Pozzoli in a hospital. Pozzoli was sleeping, which relieved Bergoglio because he dreaded seeing his mentor when he was near death. As Bergoglio was leaving, another priest told him that Pozzoli had woken up and was asking if Bergoglio was still there. Bergoglio told the priest to tell Pozzoli he had already left, something he later regretted:

> I don't know what came over me, if it was shyness or something else. But [if] I could "redo" that moment I would. How many times have I experienced deep pain and regret for my "lie" to [Pozzoli] when he was about to die. It was one of those moments in life (few, perhaps) that one would like to be able to live over again in order to behave differently.

Jorge Mario Bergoglio. "The Story of a Vocation." *L'Osservatore Romano*, January 3, 2014. http://vaticanresources.s3.amazonaws.com/pdf%2FING_2014_001_0301.pdf.

of death for three days after the surgery, and his recovery was slow and painful.

Bergoglio was in excruciating pain daily while nurses drained his lung and bandaged the wound. Bergoglio struggled to deal with the pain until a visit from Sister Dolores, a nun who had helped him prepare for his first communion. As she visited his bedside, Bergoglio said, "She told me something that really struck me and gave me much peace: 'Keep imitating Jesus.'"[22] Remembering that Jesus Christ had suffered greatly during his life and even died by crucifixion made it easier for Bergoglio to endure his own pain.

Bergoglio's calling to be a priest changed during his recovery. There are two types of priests—those who serve in a diocese (a district under the supervision of a bishop) and those who join an order of priests. Unlike diocesan priests, order priests live together as a community and devote themselves to specific missions each order adopts. The Society of Jesus, whose members are known as Jesuits, is one of the most respected orders by both Catholics and non-Catholics. They are known for spreading the Catholic faith worldwide, teaching in high schools and colleges, engaging in intellectual research, and fostering social justice. During his illness, Bergoglio began to consider joining an order and eventually decided to become a Jesuit. In an interview with the Jesuit magazine *America* after he became pope, Francis explained his choice:

> I wanted something more. But I did not know what. [Three] things in particular struck me about the Society: the missionary spirit, community and discipline. And this is strange, because I am a really, really undisciplined person. But their discipline, the way they manage their time—these things struck me so much.[23]

Bergoglio's health improved enough by November to return to school but he was not able to join the Society of Jesus until March 11, 1958, when the Jesuits admitted a new class of novitiates. It would be fifteen years more until Bergoglio would be a full-fledged Jesuit.

Creating a Jesuit

The path to becoming a Jesuit includes many years devoted to higher education and work in churches, schools, and other Jesuit facilities. Future Jesuits also spend a great deal of time strengthening their faith and spirituality, their personal relationship with God. This long period of what is called formation has two purposes—to allow candidates to discover if they are suited for religious life and to enable the order to determine if the can-

The Society of Jesus

On August 15, 1534, Ignatius of Loyola, along with six other college students, founded the Society of Jesus, whose members are known as Jesuits. Pope Paul III allowed the group to become a religious order in 1540. Ignatius was born on October 23, 1491, in Spain. He was wounded while fighting for Spain against France in the Battle of Pamplona in 1521. While recovering from his wounds, Ignatius read religious books that inspired him to dedicate his life to God. Pope Gregory XV declared Ignatius a saint on March 12, 1622. The Jesuits first became famous for introducing the Catholic faith to countries around the world. They brought Catholicism to India, Japan, China, and South America in the sixteenth century and North America in the seventeenth century. They are nicknamed "God's Soldiers" because of their founder's military background and their willingness to go anywhere and perform any task. Jesuits today are the largest religious order, with nearly 12,300 priests. The order performs many tasks including mission work in many developing countries but is best known in the field of education. Jesuits operate more than 160 schools around the world including U.S. universities such as Marquette, Fordham, and Georgetown. Many Jesuits have advanced college degrees and are renowned for their intellectual accomplishments in various fields.

didates have the necessary talent and psychological and moral makeup to become Jesuits.

Bergoglio's first step in formation was a two-year novitiate in Casa Loyola, a Jesuit facility in Padre Hurtado, Chile. Bergoglio and other young men from throughout South America, who at this stage are called novices, studied history, Latin, and Greek—the Roman Catholic mass then was said in Latin and Greek helped them study the Bible. Novices spent most of their time the first year doing spiritual exercises created by the order's founder, St. Ignatius of Loyola. They learned to pray, meditate, and review their daily actions so they would become better people and be able to serve God more effectively.

Even after Bergoglio entered the diocesan seminary in 1956, his mother for several years disliked his decision to become a priest. Regina finally relented in her opposition when Bergoglio began his novitiate and visited him even though it was a long trip to Chile. His grandmother Rosa, however, had supported him from the start. When Bergoglio told her he wanted to be a priest she responded, "Well, if God has called you, blessed be."[24]

Father Juan Valdés and Bergoglio were novices together at Casa Loyola. Valdés has fond memories of the future pope: "[He

Bergoglio earned a degree in theology in 1970 from the Church of the Colegio del Salvador in Buenos Aires, Argentina.

was] unpretentious in appearance, rather simple, but with a force in his words like the man of prayer he is. He was lucid, somewhat shy, with a sense of humor, but also quite talkative at the same time."[25] Valdés also said Bergoglio was a hard worker but enjoyed sports, including swimming.

After two years, Bergoglio took his first vows as a Jesuit on March 12, 1960. The vows were for poverty (any money Jesuits earn goes to the order), chastity, and obedience to the order and the pope. Bergoglio in the next decade continued his education and taught in Jesuit schools before being ordained a priest. Bergoglio earned degrees in philosophy from San Miguel Seminary in 1963 and theology from Colegio del Salvador in 1970; both schools were in Buenos Aires. In 1964 and 1965, Bergoglio taught literature and psychology at Colegio de la Inmaculada Concepción in Santa Fe, Argentina, and in 1966 he taught those subjects at the Colegio del Salvador secondary school in Buenos Aires.

Bergoglio enjoyed teaching. But his first year was difficult because he had never taught literature, which forced him to spend an entire summer preparing to teach the course. Although Bergoglio had never taught young people, he quickly mastered the knack of holding their attention and making them excited about learning.

Teacher Bergoglio

One of Bergoglio's students in Santa Fe was Jorge Milia, today a well-known Argentine writer. Milia said he and his classmates were tough to handle: "We were a group of rebellious adolescents, in full hormonal turmoil, hankering and hungry for anything new. We had no desire to study."[26] But Milia said the young Jesuit tamed them by making class enjoyable. Milia said that when the class discussed difficult, dreary literary passages, Bergoglio would often switch gears by reciting poetry that was so dramatic it would move them. Pope Francis today still likes to quote snippets of poetry in interviews and speeches.

Bergoglio also came up with inventive ways to help his students learn, including having them take turns teaching

Jorge Luis Borges, Argentina's most famous novelist, was persuaded by Bergoglio to lecture a class he was teaching in 1965.

A Flexible Teacher

Pope Francis has never been afraid to do things his way. When Jorge Mario Bergoglio taught literature before being ordained a priest, he realized his teenage students were not thrilled studying some of the required classic poems and books. Unlike many teachers, Bergoglio decided the best way to teach his students to love literature was to let his students read material they enjoyed:

> It was a bit risky [but] I decided [to] teach the authors the boys liked the most. [And] by reading these things they acquired a taste in literature, poetry, and we went on to other authors. And that was for me a great experience. I completed the program, but in an unstructured way—that is, not ordered according to what we expected in the beginning, but in an order that came naturally by reading these authors. And this mode befitted me: I did not like to have a rigid schedule, but rather I liked to know where we had to go with the readings, with a rough sense of where we were headed.

Antonio Spadaro. "A Big Heart Open to God." *America*, September 30, 2013. http://americamagazine.org/pope-francis-interview.

the subject, doing their own creative writing, and putting on plays. He was also flexible about assignments. When Bergoglio taught *El Cid*, an epic poem about a legendary Spanish military leader, his students asked if they could use a version by Antonio Machado. Bergoglio granted permission even though he knew why they preferred Machado: "The boys liked to find risqué things in Machado and competed to see who could find the most. I let them."[27]

Jorge Luis Borges is Argentina's most famous novelist. His works were difficult for Bergoglio's students to understand because Borges was one of the creators of magical realism, a South

American literary style that blends fantasy and reality. In 1965 Bergoglio contacted Borges and persuaded him to lecture his class, something unheard-of for someone of his literary stature. Borges helped the students publish their work in a book titled *Original Stories,* and the famous author even wrote a foreword for the book.

Milia, who wanted to be a writer, was ecstatic to meet Borges. At the same time, Milia admitted it was odd to see the friendship that developed between the twenty-eight-year-old Jesuit and the sixty-eight-year-old Borges, an agnostic. Milia has written, however, that "Borges must undoubtedly have noticed the young Bergoglio's intelligence and charm. . . . What is certain [is] that both felt a special human and intellectual respect for one another; an appreciation for one another that is different from friendship but which—like friendship—involves knowledge and admiration for the other person."[28]

Although students nicknamed Bergoglio *carucha,* Argentine slang for "the face," they knew the grim facial expressions he made in reaction to their classroom antics were a facade, and they liked him. For his part, Bergoglio once wrote, "I loved them very much," and he even thanked them "for all the good they did me, particularly for the way they taught me how to be more a brother than a father."[29]

Bergoglio in 1967 went back to being a student himself to study theology. When Bergoglio finished his degree in theology two years later, he was ordained a priest. However, during the long period of preparation for the priesthood, something happened to Bergoglio that almost derailed his decision to become a priest.

Resisting Temptation

Perhaps the biggest sacrifice priests make in their personal lives is their vow of celibacy. Bergoglio has written that at one point when he was studying to become a priest he became so attracted to a woman that he briefly thought about abandoning religious life: "When I was a seminarian, I was enchanted by a young woman at my uncle's wedding. I was surprised by her beauty, the

The Pope's Girlfriend

Jorge Mario Bergoglio, the future Pope Francis, had a normal, happy childhood while growing up in Flores, a neighborhood in Buenos Aires, Argentina. When Bergoglio was elected pope on March 13, 2013, journalists from around the world flocked to Flores to interview people who remembered him. One childhood friend the media found was seventy-seven-year-old Amalia Damonte. She soon became known as the "pope's girlfriend" in news stories when she told reporters that when Francis was twelve years old he told her he wanted to marry her. Jorge even wrote Amalia a letter in which he boldly announced his intentions: "I remember perfectly that he had drawn me a little white house, which had a red roof, and it said 'this is what I'll buy when we marry.'"[1] Damonte said the letter shocked her mother, who vowed to keep the youngsters apart and the childish romance never went any further. Damonte also said Jorge wrote in the letter "that if I didn't say yes, he would have to become a priest. Luckily for him, I said no!"[2]

1. Michael Warren. "Pope's Former Neighbor Recalls His 'Love Letter.'" AP, March 15, 2013. http://bigstory.ap.org/article/popes-former-neighbor-recalls-his-love-letter.

2. Damien Fletcher. "'Luckily for Him, I Said No!' Pope's Childhood Sweetheart Rejected His Marriage Proposal." *Daily Mirror* [London], March 15, 2013. www.mirror.co.uk/news/world-news/pope-francis-proposed-childhood-sweetheart-1764744.

When Bergoglio was twelve years old, he asked his childhood friend Amalia Damonte—seen decades later in front of her home in Buenos Aires, Argentina—to marry him.

clarity of her intellect. [When] I returned to the seminary after the wedding, I could not pray during the entire week because when I prepared to pray, the woman appeared in my mind."[30]

Bergoglio briefly explained how the woman affected him in a book he co-wrote in 2010. *On Heaven And Earth* is an extended discussion about religion between Bergoglio and Abraham Skorka, a Jewish rabbi and close friend from Buenos Aires. Bergoglio did not explain when the incident occurred, but he wrote that some men who want to be priests experience similar temptations because it is normal for men to be attracted to women.

For Bergoglio, his fascination with the woman actually strengthened his decision to become a priest because it forced him to pray to God about his future. That made Bergoglio realize that serving God was what he desired with all his heart. As a result, he continued his studies in the seminary and on December 31, 1969, he was ordained a priest.

On his ordination day Bergoglio's grandmother gave him a letter he still carries with him today. Rosa Bergoglio had actually written it two years earlier because she had feared she might die before her beloved grandson was ordained. Rosa wrote to Bergoglio, "On this beautiful day on which you hold Christ our savior in your consecrated hands, and on which a broad path to a deeper apostolate is opening up before you, I bequeath to you this humble gift of very little material but great spiritual value."[31]

The gift she offered was spiritual advice. Rosa wished him a long and happy life but said that if he ever faced a deep and troubling problem, he could survive it with his faith in God. In just a few more years, Bergoglio would need to use that advice to survive the most difficult period in his life as a priest.

Chapter 3

Bishop Bergoglio

Even after being ordained a priest, Jorge Mario Bergoglio was still not a full member of the Society of Jesus. In 1970 and part of 1971, Bergoglio was sent to the Jesuit University of Alcalá de Henares near Madrid, Spain, for the final part of Jesuit formation, known as tertianship. He spent the year studying Jesuit history and deepening his knowledge of and commitment to the order and spiritual tenets of founder Saint Ignatius. Bergoglio then returned to Argentina to become novice master and teach theology at the Jesuit seminary in San Miguel. The position of novice master was a great honor for such a young priest and showed how much faith his superiors had in Bergoglio's talents and intelligence. Jesuit priest James Martin has written that directing novices is critical in developing priests: "Jesuits often call the novice director the most important job in the province because one is required to have the spiritual depth and a practical mind to help often-confused novices. He's typically holy and sensible."[32] The position showed how much his superiors respected the thirty-four-year-old Bergoglio.

On April 22, 1973, Bergoglio took his final vows as a Jesuit to complete fifteen years of preparation for the order. Only three months later, the Jesuits again showed their confidence in Bergoglio's abilities. On July 31 in Buenos Aires, Jesuits elected him Provincial Superior of their Argentine Province, an administrative unit that included Argentina and neighboring Uruguay. The position was a huge honor for Bergoglio. But the six years the

newly minted Jesuit held the position would be the most difficult and controversial of his life.

Bergoglio Makes Mistakes

At the age of thirty-six, Bergoglio was young and inexperienced
for a position in which he made decisions affecting more than
two hundred Jesuits and the work they did. Bergoglio began
visiting and overseeing schools, houses where Jesuits lived, and
other projects Jesuits operated.

Despite his youth, Bergoglio impressed fellow Jesuits with
his charisma, austere personal habits, and dedication to God.

*Bergoglio's tenure as Provincial Superior of the Argentine
Province was more conservative than his predecessor's.
One of his mandates was to have Jesuits wear white clerical
collars at all times.*

But Bergoglio's tenure was controversial because he was more conservative than his predecessor, Father Dick O'Farrell, who had introduced liberal policies including allowing students and priests to occasionally wear casual clothing. Bergoglio made it mandatory for Jesuits to wear white clerical collars that identified them as priests. He also ordered theology teachers to use an older text written in Latin. The switch created confusion. Younger Jesuits had not been taught Latin, because since the 1960s, the church has permitted priests to say mass in their native languages instead of Latin so people can better understand mass.

Bergoglio also prohibited teaching liberation theology, which claimed that the teachings of Jesus Christ justified political opposition against governments that failed to alleviate social injustices like poverty. He did that because Pope John Paul II had rejected "this idea of Christ as a political figure, a revolutionary."[33] Poverty was such a severe problem in South America that some priests adopted this radical theology to help the poor. Bergoglio believed eliminating poverty was a just cause but rejected political opposition to accomplish that goal.

How Bergoglio made decisions also antagonized some Jesuits. Bergoglio's inexperience led him to make decisions by himself without consulting the people they affected. After becoming pope, Francis admitted in an interview that he had made many mistakes as provincial: "My style of government as a Jesuit at the beginning had many faults. . . . I had to deal with difficult situations, and I made my decisions abruptly and by myself. . . . My authoritarian and quick manner of making decisions led me to have serious problems and to be accused of being ultraconservative."[34] Bergoglio's time heading the province was also complicated by political upheaval in Argentina. This tumultuous period was known as *Guerra Sucia* (Dirty War).

A Time of Bloodshed

The military seized political control of Argentina six times in the twentieth century. The last takeover was in 1976, when General Jorge Videla overthrew President Isabel Perón. Videla

A banner with pictures of some of the people who were "disappeared" between 1976 and 1983 is displayed at a 2007 commemoration in Buenos Aires, Argentina.

governed like a dictator. He was merciless in attacking anyone he suspected of opposing him, and Argentine soldiers and secret police arrested, tortured, and killed thousands of people without benefit of trial. Victims included Communists, journalists, students, labor union members, and at least 130 priests. Many people who were illegally seized were never seen again and became known as *desaparecidos* (the disappeared). The Argentine government estimates the number of Dirty War victims at 22,000, but other estimates run as high as 30,000. Argentina became a democracy again in 1983, when Videla was defeated in a bid for re-election as president.

In the years following the Dirty War, Argentines criticized religious leaders who had not publicly opposed Videla even though they would have risked death to do it. Bergoglio was among those criticized for this failure of courage. What people did not know was that Bergoglio had worked secretly to save the lives of many people. Attorney Alicia Oliveira, renowned for her bravery in opposing Videla, was a friend of Bergoglio during this dark period of Argentine history. Oliveira has said Bergoglio hid or helped many people escape capture and death: "I used to go to the [Jesuit] retreat house, and I recall that many of the meals served there were farewell dinners for people who Father Jorge smuggled out of the country."[35] Oliveira said Bergoglio once gave his own identity card and clerical clothing to a man who resembled him so he could flee Argentina.

Bergoglio has been accused of helping the government arrest Jesuit priests Francisco Jalics and Father Orlando Yorio, who worked with the poor in areas of Buenos Aires called *villas miserias* (villas of misery). Bergoglio has denied that claim, and Jalics himself has said Bergoglio played no part in their arrest. As provincial, however, Bergoglio did order the priests to stop living and working with the poor because he feared they would be imprisoned. Some people claim government officials felt free to arrest Jalics and Yorio in May 1976 after they learned of Bergoglio's order. Bergoglio sought their release but his appeal failed, as did those of religious leaders in similar situations. Until being released in October 1976, the priests were interrogated and brutally tortured about possible antigovernment activities. The

Bergoglio's List

Schindler's List is a book about how Oskar Schindler saved 1,200 Jews during World War II. *Bergoglio's List* by Nello Scavo details how Father Jorge Mario Bergoglio saved hundreds of people from death or imprisonment during Argentina's Dirty War. Gonzalo Mosca was a Uruguayan who fled to Argentina to escape his own country's dictators. Mosca contacted Bergoglio, who hid him in a seminary near Buenos Aires and arranged an airline ticket to take him to safety in Brazil. In a 2013 interview after Bergoglio became pope, Mosca said he was stunned Bergoglio was not afraid to help him: "He made me wonder if he really understood the trouble he was getting into. If they grabbed us together, they would have marched us both off." Bergoglio also helped his old chemical factory boss Esther Balestrino de Careaga, a Communist. Bergoglio hid Communist books she owned in a Jesuit library because he feared she would be arrested for having them. When de Careaga began working publicly to help people who disappeared, the government seized and killed her by dropping her from a helicopter into the sea. After her body washed ashore, Bergoglio had her buried in the garden of a church.

Debora Rey. "Survivors: Pope Francis Saved Many in Dirty Wars." *New Haven Register*, March 13, 2014. www.nhregister.com/general-news/20140314/survivors-pope-francis-saved-many-during-dirty-wars.

government claimed it arrested the priests for associating with violent guerrilla fighters opposed to Videla. But Yorio said that after five days of torture a soldier told him the real reason he and Jalics were imprisoned. Yorio said the soldier told him, "We know you're not violent [but] you've gone to live with the poor. Living with the poor unites them. Uniting the poor is subversion."[36]

Adolfo Pérez Esquivel was imprisoned and tortured for fighting for human rights in Argentina. In 1980, Esquivel won the Nobel Peace Prize for his courageous actions during the Dirty War and for helping afterward to uncover details of atrocities Videla's government committed. Esquivel states that Bergoglio never cooperated with Videla:

> There were bishops who were accomplices, but not Bergoglio. There is no link relating him to the dictatorship. Bergoglio is questioned because it is said he did not do enough to get two priests out of prison while he was the superior of the Jesuits. But I know personally that many bishops requested the military junta to release prisoners and priests but they were not heeded.[37]

When Bergoglio's six-year tenure ended in 1979, he was named rector, or head, of Colegio Máximo, a Jesuit college in San José, Argentina. Before starting the new job, Bergoglio spent the first three months of 1980 learning English at the Jesuit Milltown Institute of Theology and Philosophy in Dublin, Ireland.

A Change of Heart

Upon his return to Argentina, Bergoglio began teaching at Colegio Máximo, which was located about 18 miles (30km) south of Buenos Aires. Bergoglio enjoyed academic life and said mass and performed other priestly duties in the area. When his term as rector ended in 1986, Bergoglio spent six months at the Sankt Georgen Graduate School of Philosophy and Theology in Frankfurt, Germany, to research subjects for a doctorate in philosophy.

When Bergoglio returned to Buenos Aires, he began teaching part-time at Colegio del Salvador, a Jesuit university, and lecturing one day a week at Colegio Máximo. Even though Bergoglio was no longer a Jesuit leader, he disagreed with the way the schools were run. Many Jesuits admired Bergoglio, but he was still unpopular with others in his order because of his stormy tenure as provincial. Bergoglio began angering even more Jesuits by trying to interfere with how the schools were run. He created so much dissension that in 1990 Provincial Superior Victor Zorzín sent him to work as a confessor and spiritual director in

While studying at Colegio Máximo, Bergoglio lived in this bedroom, photographed in 2013. Later in his career, he provided refuge and safe passage to dozens of priests, seminarians, and political dissidents during the Dirty War, using the seminary as his home base.

the Jesuit community in Córdoba, which was nearly 400 miles (642km) from Buenos Aires.

In effect, Zorzín isolated Bergoglio so he could not cause any more problems. Bergoglio's diminished role with the Jesuit order and the way he was treated depressed him. In an interview after becoming pope, Francis admitted, "I lived a time of great interior crisis when I was in Córdoba."[38] Father Guillermo Marcó was Bergoglio's press spokesperson for eight years. Marcó said Bergoglio confessed to him how difficult his time in Córdoba was: "[His] own order treated him with suspicion back then, he told me. They would open his letters and fail to pass on telephone messages. He was doing a penance, as far as he was concerned. He was given very little to do. 'I thought my life was finished when I was in that place,' he said to me."[39]

During this dark period, Bergoglio began reviewing his life to understand what he had done wrong. In that time of contemplation, Bergoglio realized the mistakes he had made as provincial superior and rector. The deep regret Bergoglio feels about his poor leadership is evident in comments he made in a book published in 2010: "From a young age, life pushed me into leadership roles—as soon as I was ordained a priest, I was designated as the master of novices, and two and a half years later, of the province—and I had to learn from my errors along the way, because, to tell you the truth, I made hundreds of errors. Errors and sins."[40]

Raymond A. Schroth is a Jesuit priest who writes for *America* magazine. He believes that in Córdoba, Bergoglio used the spiritual exercises of St. Ignatius to understand what he had done wrong; one of the exercises' main tenets is to review one's actions to make sure they were correct. Argentine Rabbi Abraham Skorka, a close friend of Bergoglio, believes the future pope was able to become a better person by recognizing his mistakes: "Bergoglio has changed over the years. . . . He is a person who is learning from life [and] has changed according to his life's experience."[41]

Bergoglio's period of isolation and its resulting spiritual growth ended in an unexpected way. When it did, Bergoglio began using his new self-knowledge to become the caring administrator he had not been in the past.

Bishop Bergoglio

Although some Jesuits disliked Bergoglio, many of them admired him because of his intelligence, devotion to God, and warm personality. Bergoglio was also highly esteemed by many other Catholics including Father Ubaldo Calabresi, the pope's representative in Argentina. One of Calabresi's duties was to assess priests for the position of bishop. Bishops are administrators for a diocese or archdiocese—an area larger than a diocese—and have the power to perform special duties such as ordaining priests.

Calabresi became friends with Bergoglio and began to rely on him for advice on various issues including which priests to recommend to the pope as bishop. On May 13, 1992, the two

Bergoglio's Interfaith Relations

As archbishop of Buenos Aires, Jorge Mario Bergoglio improved relations with other religions. One of Bergoglio's best friends was Rabbi Abraham Skorka, with whom he wrote *On Heaven and Earth*. The book is a dialogue on religious and contemporary social issues as seen from the point of view of Christianity and Judaism. Bergoglio and Skorka had been having such discussions for several years before they put their thoughts on paper. In the book's introduction, Bergoglio wrote, "Dialogue is born from a respectful attitude toward the other person, from a conviction that the other person has something good to say. It supposes that we can make room in our heart for their point of view, their opinion and their proposals." Bergoglio also worked to strengthen interfaith cooperation with Muslims, evangelical Christians, and members of the Orthodox Church. The Orthodox Catholic Church—also known as the Eastern Orthodox Church—has more than 200 million members worldwide. The Orthodox Church split from the Catholic Church in 1054. In 1998, Bergoglio was named head of Orthodox Church members in Argentina because they did not have a religious figure with the authority he possessed. Bergoglio was praised for the work he did in the position.

Jorge Mario Bergoglio and Abraham Skorka. *On Heaven and Earth: Pope Francis on Faith, Family and the Church in the Twenty-First Century*. New York: Image, 2013, p. xiv.

met in Córdoba. After they had been talking for some time, Calabresi calmly told Bergoglio, "Ah, just one more thing. You have been appointed auxiliary [assistant] bishop of Buenos Aires."[42] The news stunned Bergoglio. Just seven days later, the fifty-five-year-old Bergoglio became one of five assistant bishops who helped Cardinal Antonio Quarracino oversee the vast Archdiocese of Buenos Aires.

Bergoglio was put in charge of Flores. He immersed himself again in the area of his youth by visiting churches and other Catholic sites. Bergoglio also walked endlessly through Flores, often taking along Father Marcó to help him become acquainted with people who lived there. The young priest said he was amazed Bergoglio sought his advice and wanted to learn his thoughts on various church issues.

The humility Bergoglio displayed in seeking help from Marcó showed how much he had changed. His new, more cooperative attitude in working with people helped him perform so well in his new position that on December 31, 1993, he was named vicar general, Quarracino's top aide, and on June 3, 1997, coadjutator bishop. The latter promotion ensured Bergoglio would succeed Quarracino as head of the archdiocese. When Quarracino died on February 28, 1998, Bergoglio became archbishop of Buenos Aires.

Bishop of the Slums

The Archdiocese of Buenos Aires was huge—Bergoglio was responsible for directing the work of 850 priests and meeting the needs of 2.5 million Catholics. Unlike his early years as an

Bergoglio visits a slum in Buenos Aires during his tenure as archbishop.

The Poor Knew Bergoglio

When Jorge Mario Bergoglio was elected pope in 2013, residents of the slums of Buenos Aires known as *villas miserias* (villas of misery) rejoiced. Father Juan Isasmendi, who works in one of those pockets of extreme poverty, said people were happy because they knew the new pope personally because of his many visits to such slums. Isasmendi said, "The people from the villas know Bergoglio, and when we had mass to celebrate his election, they all brought their pictures with him." When reporter John L. Allen Jr. visited those slums in April 2013 to do a story on Pope Francis, he wanted to find out if some of the poorest people in the world really had pictures of themselves with the pope. After Allen asked one woman if she had a picture, she darted into her small home made of tin and wood and came back with not one but two pictures of Bergoglio with her family.

John L. Allen Jr. "Pope Francis Gets His 'Oxygen' from the Slums." *National Catholic Reporter*, April 7, 2013. http://ncronline.org/blogs/francis-chronicles/pope-francis-gets-his-oxygen-slums.

administrator, Bergoglio governed by sharing his duties with assistant bishops, giving them freedom to do their jobs, and seeking input and counsel from them and others on most issues. In explaining his new style of governing, Bergoglio has said:

> The Lord has allowed this growth in knowledge of government through my faults and my sins. So as Archbishop of Buenos Aires, I had a meeting with the six auxiliary bishops every two weeks, and several times a year with the council of priests. They asked questions and we opened the floor for discussion. This greatly helped me to make the best decisions.[43]

One of Bergoglio's most important decisions was to increase the church's presence in the slums of Buenos Aires, where people lived in squalid conditions. Their homes were dilapidated shacks, or sometimes only cardboard boxes, without electricity or plumbing. Argentina's government mostly ignored their plight, and the areas were so dangerous that policemen often feared to enter them, which made the poor easy prey for drug dealers and other criminals.

Bergoglio quadrupled the number of priests in the *villas miserias* from six to twenty-four. One was Father Juan Isasmendi, who cites Bergoglio's bravery in defending a fellow priest. In 2009, a drug dealer threatened to kill Father Jose "Pepe" di Paola for trying to stop people from using *paco,* a cheap form of cocaine. When di Paola told Bergoglio he feared for his life, the archbishop moved quickly to protect him. Isasmendi said, "He showed up [the next day] unannounced and walked slowly throughout the entire villa as if to say, if you touch them, you touch me."[44] Bergoglio even offered to sleep in di Paola's home to protect him.

The *villas miserias* became a second home to Bergoglio, who spent time walking through them and meeting the poorest and most vulnerable people in Argentina so he could better learn how to help them. Bergoglio became known as "Bishop of the Slums" and completed the mission Jalics and Yorio had begun by improving the lives of the poor in many ways. Bergoglio helped clothe and feed the poor, educate them, and provide them with medical care. His dedication to the poor impressed many people because they were often ignored by both the government and the church.

Chapter 4

Cardinal Bergoglio

In his years as bishop and archbishop, Jorge Mario Bergoglio endeared himself to people in Buenos Aires with his simple, humble lifestyle. When Bergoglio met people, he introduced himself as "Padre (Priest) Jorge" instead of the more prestigious titles of his higher office. Instead of being chauffeured around the vast city in a car like his predecessor, Bergoglio walked, rode a bike or a bus, or took the Subterráneo de Buenos Aires, the city's underground subway system, like everyone else. During one of Bergoglio's frequent forays into the poorest areas of Buenos Aires, a visit to Our Lady of Caacupé Church, a man stood up and told Bergoglio, "I am proud of you, because when I came here with my companions on the bus I saw you sitting in one of the last seats, like one of us. I told them it was you, but no one believed me."[45]

After he became archbishop, Bergoglio declined to live in the elegant archbishop's home in Olivos, a rich suburb in which the president of Argentina also resided. Instead, Bergoglio took much more humble quarters in the archdiocesan offices in downtown Buenos Aires. His small bedroom contained a simple wooden bed, which he made himself every day, and its sparse decorations included a crucifix his grandparents had given him. Bergoglio chose another small room for his office instead of the big one other archbishops had used. He then filled that larger space with clothing and food to give to the poor. The archbishop even answered his telephone himself. Bergoglio would stay up late working and get up before dawn at 4:30 A.M. because he needed only five hours of sleep. His simple lifestyle included making his own breakfast and sometimes cooking for other priests who lived with him. Father Angel Rossi claimed, "He always cooked fantastic paella [a Spanish rice dish] for us."[46]

The humble way Bergoglio lived, the loving way he dealt with people, and his devotion to the poor did not go unnoticed outside Argentina. On February 21, 2001, Pope John Paul II made Bergoglio a cardinal. Cardinals wear red clothing as a sign of their high office. Instead of buying a red robe, Bergoglio used an old one that belonged to deceased Cardinal Antonio Quarracino. Bergoglio also asked people who wanted to go to Rome for the ceremony making him a cardinal to stay home and donate money they would have spent on the trip to the poor.

On the day Bergoglio became a cardinal, he decided to walk more than a mile to the ceremony through the streets of Rome instead of taking the limousine provided for him. Clad in scarlet

Bergoglio talks to a man while traveling on the subway in Buenos Aires, Argentina. Instead of being chauffeured, he preferred to ride public transportation or a bicycle to get around.

robes that identified him as a cardinal, Bergoglio and his aide, Father Guillermo Marcó, stopped for a cup of coffee along the way. Marcó was worried about the attention Bergoglio was getting from people, but Bergoglio smiled and told him, "Don't worry! In Rome you can walk around with a banana on your head and nobody will notice."[47]

Conservative and Compassionate

One reason for Bergoglio's elevation to cardinal was that he was considered a strict conservative on issues of church doctrine such as opposing abortion, birth control, gay marriage, and women becoming priests. John Paul II was a conservative, and during his twenty-six-year reign, which ended with his death on April 2, 2005, most priests he elevated to bishop or cardinal shared that ideology.

Bergoglio displayed his conservative side in 2010 after Argentina became the first South American country to adopt a law allowing same-sex couples the rights to marry and adopt children. Bergoglio opposed the law. In language that made him seem unfeeling toward same-sex couples, the cardinal wrote that the law had "the intention to destroy the plan of God," that marriage was between a man and woman, and that the law was promoted by "the father of lies who wants to confuse and trick the children of God."[48] The latter reference that the devil was the "father of lies" and the one tricking people made his comments seem even more rigid and out of touch with modern thought about gay rights.

Marcelo Márquez, an Argentine gay rights leader, was upset about Bergoglio's statement and wrote him a letter expressing his anger with the archbishop's stance. Within an hour after the upset activist delivered the letter to Bergoglio, the archbishop called Márquez, who was amazed at what Bergoglio said. Although Bergoglio was adamant in opposing gay marriage, Márquez said, "He told me, 'I'm in favor of gay rights and in any case, I also favor civil unions for homosexuals, but I believe that Argentina is not yet ready for a gay marriage law.'"[49] The call convinced Márquez, a Catholic who once taught theology

Demonstrators wave a gay pride flag outside Argentina's Congress building in support of a proposal to legalize same-sex marriage in 2010. Although he opposes same-sex marriage, Bergoglio is considered a moderate on gay rights.

at a Catholic seminary, that Bergoglio was actually a moderate on gay rights. Bergoglio's views were in stark contrast to his predecessor, Cardinal Quarracino, who once said homosexuals should be locked up.

The interchange between the two men showed the difference between statements Bergoglio had to make to defend church doctrine on issues like gay marriage and the more accepting and loving nature he had personally toward people involved in such issues. Bergoglio also told Márquez that he had helped many gay people deal with spiritual issues in their lives despite his own reservations about their lifestyle. Bergoglio was able to do that because, unlike some religious leaders, he has the capacity to love and accept people even when he disagrees with their beliefs or actions.

Relaxing the Rules

In August 2008, Bergoglio said mass in a Buenos Aires slum. He used that occasion to initiate a brief dialogue with those in attendance to explain his belief that the Catholic Church should never turn its back on anyone. Bergoglio first asked the crowd if only good people can come to church—their response was no. He then asked if there was room in the church for the wicked—their answer was yes. Bergoglio finished his lesson in tolerance by saying: "Do we chase someone away here because he is bad? No, on the contrary, we welcome him with more affection. And who taught us this? Jesus taught us this. Imagine, then, how patient the heart of God is with each one of us."[50]

Bergoglio's desire to always be loving and helpful toward people led him, at times, to ignore Catholic doctrine and to help people even if they violated church rules. Father Juan Isasmendi, a priest who worked in the slums, said, "He was never rigid about the small and stupid stuff."[51] One of the "stupid" things Isasmendi referred to was that priests were not supposed to baptize children of unwed or divorced mothers because they were not living in a state of marriage acceptable to the Catholic Church.

In 2009, Bergoglio showed he did not hold such rules sacred when he baptized seven children of a woman who had them with two different men. The woman herself had approached Bergoglio when he was saying mass in a poor area. She told him she wanted her children baptized even though she admitted she was sinful. Despite her lack of a church-approved marital status, Bergoglio agreed to baptize them. Bergoglio even hosted the ceremony in the chapel of the archdiocesan chancery where he lived and served sandwiches and soda to her family afterward. The woman was so full of gratitude she told him, "Father, I can't believe it, you make me feel important," to which he replied, "But . . . where do I come in, it's Jesus who makes you important."[52]

In an interview not long afterward with an Italian magazine, Bergoglio explained why he helped the woman. He said refusing to baptize them would have penalized innocent children for something they had not done. Bergoglio also said he approves

Bringing God to People

As archbishop, Jorge Mario Bergoglio believed the Catholic Church should try to make it easier for people to connect with God. In a 2007 interview with an Italian magazine, Bergoglio said that included creating places where people could get spiritual help, even if these places were not churches:

> Our sociologists of religion tell us that the influence of a parish [church] has a radius of six hundred meters. In Buenos Aires there are about two thousand meters between one parish and the next. So I then told the priests: "If you can, rent a garage and, if you find some willing layman, let him go there! Let him be with those people a bit, do a little [religious education] and even give communion if they ask him." A parish priest said to me: "But Father, if we do this the people then won't come to church." "But why?" I asked him: "Do they come to mass now?" "No," he answered. And so! Coming out of oneself is also coming out from the fenced garden of one's own convictions, considered irremovable, if they risk becoming an obstacle, if they close the horizon that is also of God.

Sefania Falasca. "An Interview with Cardinal Jorge Mario Bergoglio." *30 Days*, November 2007. www.30giorni.it/articoli_id_16457_l3.htm.

of lay (nonreligious) people baptizing infants when no priest is present, a problem in parts of rural Argentina because there are not enough priests to serve sparsely populated areas. Bergoglio said priests could complete the ceremony later by anointing babies with holy oil. The practice is common in South America, where men and women who initiate baptisms are called *bautizadores* (baptizers).

Bergoglio's belief that everyone is worthy of God's love also led him to break an unwritten rule in a ceremony performed on

Pope Francis kisses the foot of a man while performing a traditional Washing of the Feet in 2014 at a center for disabled people in Rome, Italy, continuing a break with tradition he began as cardinal.

the Thursday before Easter, which is known as Holy Thursday. On that day, bishops wash the feet of twelve priests in an act of humility symbolic of Jesus Christ, who washed the feet of his twelve disciples on that same day. Bergoglio broke the tradition

of washing the feet of only priests. Instead, he chose lay people including the poor, prison inmates, and AIDS patients, who many in the church would have condemned for how they had lived.

But for Bergoglio, no group of people was more worthy or deserving of help than the poor. His personal experiences dealing with slum dwellers had shown him how poverty made their lives harder by denying them things most people take for granted, like adequate food, housing, and medical care. Eventually, Bergoglio's championing of the poor made him a political enemy of the Argentine government.

The Voice of the Poor

Widespread poverty has often been a problem in South American countries because of a lack of good jobs and economic opportunities. But in 2001, that problem grew to historic proportions in Argentina. Before the military takeover in the 1970s, only about 7 percent of Argentines had lived in poverty. During the brutal reign of the military in the 1970s and 1980s, the country's economy weakened and many people lost their jobs when some 400,000 companies went out of business.

Argentina's economy was so weak that it had to begin borrowing money from other nations so it could continue to govern. Government debt grew so large that by December 2001 Argentina could no longer repay even the interest it owed on $94 billion in loans. The result was a collapse of the country's economy that eventually left more than 50 percent of Argentinians living in poverty.

In order to achieve economic stability, the Argentine government cut spending. But when the government drastically reduced services to the poor, Bergoglio began using the moral authority of his position as cardinal to attack officials for failing to do enough for the Argentinians that needed government

In 2001 half of Argentineans lived in poverty, and many were forced to move to slums such as these outside Buenos Aires.

help the most. Bergoglio condemned Argentina's government in strong language, even claiming it had sinned by ignoring the poor: "I would say that, deep down [not helping the poor] is a problem of sin. Argentina has been living a sinful existence because it has not taken responsibility for those who have no food or work [and it thus] shows a lack of personal conscience."[53]

His powerful comments angered government leaders, including Néstor Carlos Kirchner, who was president from 2003 until his death in 2007, and Cristina Fernández de Kirchner, who succeeded her husband as president when he died. Although the Kirchners had worked hard to improve the economy and help the poor, Bergoglio believed they had not done enough. He also criticized them for underreporting the size of the problem by using statistics that showed fewer people living in poverty than was actually the case.

Oscar Aguad, an Argentine political figure, said relations between Bergoglio and the Kirchners deteriorated so much that "Néstor Kirchner even said that Bergoglio was the head of the opposition."[54] One way Bergoglio angered the Kirchners was with remarks he made at the annual *Te Deum* (To the Lord) mass

"Poverty of Knowledge"

Cardinal Jorge Mario Bergoglio helped write the report issued after the Fifth Latin American Bishops Conference in Aparecida, Brazil. Much of the report deals with the problem of economic inequality that persists in Latin America. However, the report also acknowledges that a lack of knowledge about modern technology and a lack of skills to use technology are two of the factors that keep many Latin Americans in a state of poverty:

> Led by a tendency that prizes profit and stimulates competition, globalization entails a process of concentration of power and wealth in the hands of a few, not only of physical and monetary resources, but especially of information and human resources. The upshot is the exclusion of all those not sufficiently trained and informed, thereby augmenting the inequalities that sadly characterize our continent and that keep large numbers of people in poverty. Today poverty means poverty of knowledge and of use of, and access to, new technologies. Hence, business people must take on their responsibility of creating more sources of employment and investing in overcoming this new poverty.

Text of the report issued by bishops attending the Fifth Latin American Bishops Conference May 13–31, 2007, in Aparecida, Brazil. www.celam.org/aparecida/Ingles.pdf.

held each May 25. By tradition, Bergoglio, as head of the Catholic Church in Buenos Aires, was free to criticize government officials for what was wrong with society. Bergoglio enraged the Kirchners by vigorously attacking government officials for not only ignoring the poor but for corruption and other failings.

In retaliation, Néstor Kirchner in 2005 began moving the ceremony outside of Buenos Aires. And in 2008, Cristina de Kirchner ended a 198-year-old tradition of having the archbishop preside over the ceremony. Instead, she turned it into an ecumenical event that included leaders from other religions, even though Argentina is 90 percent Catholic.

Bergoglio, however, refused to quit criticizing government inadequacy. He once contrasted the way the government treated the poor with how the church helped them by stating, "We are tired of systems that produce poor people so that then the church can support them."[55] Argentina's continued failure to help the poor frustrated Bergoglio. As he continued to ponder solutions to poverty, Bergoglio began to consider why there were so many poor people in Argentina as well as in other countries. Bergoglio finally decided that inequalities in the global economic system were one of the root causes of poverty. He began to speak out against them.

Social Justice

The Catholic Church's concept of social justice includes the belief that meeting the needs of the poorest and most vulnerable

Thousands of unemployed Argentineans march in Buenos Aires in 2002 demanding food for the city's schools.

Helping a Widow

Jerónimo José Podestá in 1962 was named bishop of the Catholic diocese of Avellaneda near Buenos Aires. Four years later Podestá began a relationship with Clelia Luro, his secretary, who was a divorced mother with six children. One year later, the Church suspended Podestá from performing the duties of a priest such as saying mass but did not defrock him, which would mean he was no longer a priest. Podestá and Luro married, and both became controversial for advocating for the right of priests to marry. When Podestá became ill and was dying, no priests would bless him as they normally would someone who was sick. Podestá called Archbishop Jorge Mario Bergoglio for help. And Bergoglio, despite his opposition to marriage for priests, agreed to see Podestá. Luro said:

> Nobody from the Church came near us, but when Bergoglio realized he was hospitalized, he talked to him by phone. And when they moved him into therapy, [Bergoglio] put everything aside and came to bring him the anointing of the sick. [I] know what it must have meant to Jerónimo for a [high church official] to accompany him and be praying with him.

> Luro said after her husband died, Bergoglio would call her every Sunday to make sure she was all right. He continued to be attentive to her after becoming pope.

Roly Villani. "Francis 'Will Be a Great Pope': Clelia Luro de Podestá Weighs In on the New Pontiff." *Tiempo Argentino*, March 17, 2013. http://iglesiadescalza.blogspot.com/2013/03/francis-will-be-great-pope-clelia-luro.html.

members of society is of utmost importance. Bergoglio came to believe that the global economy was responsible for much of the world's poverty because it made a minority of people wealthy while dooming many more people to lives of bare subsistence.

During the economic crisis in Argentina, Bergoglio claimed that rich people had failed to do enough to help the poor because they were more worried about maintaining their "privileges [and] their share of ill-gotten gain [while Argentina was] on the verge of national dissolution."[56] Bergoglio believed wealthy people were contributing to growing poverty by economic decisions they made, such as paying workers low salaries and influencing governments to pass policies that favored them over the poor.

Bergoglio carried this message to the Latin American Bishops Conference held in May 2007, in Aparecida, Brazil. In an address to 162 bishops from Latin America, the Caribbean, the United States, and Canada, Bergoglio claimed that growing economies in Latin America were failing to benefit more people because "We live in the most unequal part of the world, which [in recent years] has grown the most yet reduced misery the least. The unjust distribution of goods persists, creating a situation of social sin that cries out to Heaven and limits the possibilities of a fuller life for so many of our brothers."[57]

The bishops issued a report after the conference stating the church's position on many aspects of life in Latin America. The report's view of economic inequality reflected Bergoglio's beliefs on poverty and concluded, "[Catholics must work for] the well-being of every human person. Structures must be created that serve a social, economic and political order in which inequalities are overcome and in which opportunities are open for every person."[58]

Bergoglio's involvement in the conference heightened his profile in the Catholic Church globally. His fierce defense of the poor began to make people believe Bergoglio could one day be worthy of becoming pope.

Chapter 5

Bergoglio Becomes Pope Francis

Popes and presidents are both elected, but the process of electing a pope is quite different than presidential campaigns in which millions of people cast votes for candidates. Popes are elected in a secret papal conclave by cardinals who are younger than eighty. The cardinals all know each other, even

Pope Francis waves to the crowd from the central balcony of St. Peter's Basilica in the Vatican—as is traditional for a new pope's first public appearance—on March 13, 2013.

if only slightly, so their votes are based on what they know personally about *papabili*, a Latin phrase for cardinals considered worthy to be pope. In his seven years as archbishop of Buenos Aires, Jorge Mario Bergoglio had emerged as a papal candidate for his work championing the poor, his unyielding defense of conservative church doctrine on issues such as abortion and birth control, and his charismatic personality.

When Pope John Paul II died on April 2, 2005, Bergoglio's name was mentioned in news stories about *papabili*. Gerard O'Connell, an Irish journalist who had written extensively about the Catholic Church, praised Bergoglio and claimed he was a strong contender: "He's the most deeply spiritual man in the College of Cardinals [the name for cardinals electing a pope]. He stands out—he is a man of God. Ordinary people love him. His sermons are literary pieces and he's a leading moral authority in Argentina."[59] O'Connell and other journalists also speculated that it might be time to elect the first Latin American pope because Latin America was home to more than 40 percent of the world's Catholics.

Not-So-Secret Voting

Choosing John Paul's successor was difficult because he was considered one of the most important figures of the twentieth century—he helped end communism in his native Poland—and he was the most popular pope the world had ever known. John Paul had steered the Catholic Church on a conservative course by continuing the church's opposition to birth control, ordination of women, and ending celibacy for priests, even though more and more Catholics around the world had begun supporting such liberal changes. German Cardinal Joseph Ratzinger, one of the pope's closest advisors, was a pre-conclave favorite to continue John Paul's conservative legacy.

The voting started April 18 in Rome when 115 cardinals from fifty-two countries entered the Sistine Chapel. Papal voting has traditionally been a secret process. To ensure that secrecy, cardinals are sequestered, or isolated, in the chapel, where they vote, and in the nearby Casa Santa Marta, a hotel where they eat and sleep. After two days of voting, Ratzinger was elected and assumed the name Pope Benedict XVI.

After the election, an unidentified cardinal broke tradition by releasing voting details to an Italian journalist. When the story spread around the world, millions of people were surprised to discover that Bergoglio had been second in voting. On the first ballot Ratzinger got forty-seven votes, Bergoglio ten, and

Swiss Guards stand at the entrance to Casa Santa Marta, where Cardinals stay during a conclave and where Pope Francis currently has his living quarters, in March 2013.

no other cardinal more than nine. Cardinals only voted once the first day. In the second ballot the next day, Ratzinger tallied sixty-five votes and Bergoglio thirty-five. Ratzinger in the third ballot received seventy-two votes, five fewer than the two-thirds majority needed to win, and Bergoglio forty. The cardinals then ate lunch.

Although Bergoglio was gaining votes, it was apparent he did not want to be pope. The cardinal who revealed the voting details described the anguished look on Bergoglio's face when he realized he could be elected: "The suffering face, as if he were begging: 'God don't do this to me.'"[60] During the lunch break, Bergoglio let other cardinals know he did not want the job, and on the fourth ballot Ratzinger was elected. His total of eighty-four, however, was far lower than the ninety-nine votes John Paul II received in 1978, especially because the conclave electing John Paul II had only 111 voting cardinals.

Bergoglio, who had once said, "I'm a native of the city and I wouldn't know what to do with myself outside the city,"[61] heaved a sigh of relief and returned to his beloved Buenos Aires. His return home, however, would only last eight years.

Pope Benedict XVI

Unlike John Paul II, Pope Benedict XVI had little personal charm. His election had not excited most Catholics, and he failed to increase his popularity because of several scandals involving the church and things he did that insulted other religions.

As a cardinal, Ratzinger since 2001 had headed the church's agency that dealt with allegations of sexual abuse of children by priests. He was repeatedly criticized during those years and as pope for failing to forcefully deal with the problem. In 2010, a criminal investigation began into the Vatican Bank in Rome, the church's financial arm, over allegations of corruption by employees and illegalities in how the bank transferred money. Benedict was personally embarrassed in 2012 when it was uncovered that Paolo Gabriele, his butler, had given a reporter confidential letters and documents Benedict had received concerning the bank scandal.

In 2006, Benedict insulted Muslims by citing a quotation offensive to Islam, touching off angry protests and violence against Christians in Muslim countries. Benedict in 2007 angered other Christian faiths by claiming the Catholic Church was the only true church founded by Jesus Christ. In 2008, Benedict allowed use of an ancient Good Friday prayer that contained negative references to Judaism. One year later, Benedict further angered Jews by reinstating an English bishop who had denied that millions of Jews died in the Holocaust. Papal personnel had to apologize for Benedict's many miscues and try to explain that he had never meant to insult anyone by his words or actions.

The pope's age, the demands of his job, and failing health—his hearing deteriorated and he lost sight in his left eye—wore Benedict down physically. On February 11, 2013, Benedict

Pope Benedict XVI meets Cardinal Bergoglio at the Vatican in 2007.

His Enemies Attacked Him

Shortly before the start of the 2005 papal conclave, Marcelo Parrilli, a human rights lawyer in Buenos Aires, Argentina, filed a lawsuit against Cardinal Jorge Mario Bergoglio. The lawsuit tried to resurrect the quarter-century old allegations that Bergoglio in 1976 had helped government officials kidnap two Jesuit priests—Orlando Yorio and Francisco Jalics. Father Guillermo Marcó, Bergoglio's spokesman, said of the charges, "This is old slander. [There] is no proof." Marcó said the claims had already been proven false. Bergoglio for years had denied helping the military dictator find and arrest the two priests. Furthermore, many people who had been victims during the Dirty War period or opposed the dictatorship had come forward to say Bergoglio was innocent of the charges. The claims had no effect on the voting by cardinals. Argentine journalist Elisabetta Piqué, who has been a friend of Bergoglio since 2001 and has written a biography of him, claimed the attack came from the cardinal's political enemies. Bergoglio had angered many Argentine politicians including Presidents Néstor Kirchner and his wife, Cristina Fernández de Kirchner, who succeeded him, because he complained the government was not doing enough to help the poor. Some politicians also criticized Bergoglio for not supporting gay marriage.

Jorge Covarrubias. "Complaint on '76 Kidnappings Accuses Potential Contender." *Boston Globe*, April 17, 2005. www.boston.com/news/world/latinamerica/articles/2005/04/17/complaint_on_76_kidnappings_accuses_potential_contender.

stunned the world by announcing he would resign on February 28. Benedict, who on April 16 would turn eighty-six, said, "After having repeatedly examined my conscience before God, I have come to the certainty that my strengths, due to an advanced age, are no longer suited to [serve as pope]."[62] On February 28,

Benedict became the first pope to step down since Pope Gregory XII in 1415. What happened next would also be historic and surprise the world.

Another Papal Conclave

After Benedict's election, Bergoglio returned to Buenos Aires to resume his duties as archbishop. As part of his continuing efforts to improve interfaith relations, Bergoglio co-authored a book and appeared on a television show with his good friend Rabbi Abraham Skorka. Both efforts were dialogues on how they viewed the Bible and various religious and social issues from the perspectives of Christianity and Judaism. When Benedict created dissension with other religions, Bergoglio did not hesitate to criticize the pope. Bergoglio said the pope's comment on Islam had threatened to destroy two decades of work by Pope John Paul II to improve relations with Muslims. Bergoglio also took a harder stance than Benedict against priests who abused children and harshly criticized church officials who concealed the abuse.

Benedict had been criticized throughout his reign. But he was hailed for his decision to resign because many people thought it would help the Catholic Church, which was losing followers and whose image had been tarnished by his conduct. The cardinals who traveled to Rome to elect Benedict's successor knew their choice would be important because the next pope had to revitalize the church's global image, inspire Catholics, and convince Catholics who had left the church to return.

As the March 12 start of the papal conclave approached, news stories speculated on who would be chosen. John L. Allen Jr., a journalist knowledgeable about church affairs, wrote profiles of possible popes. In one article, Allen said Bergoglio would be a strong candidate because of his "reputation for personal simplicity" and "as a genuinely spiritual soul, and a man of deep prayer."[63] However, Allen said Bergoglio's age—he was seventy-six—hurt his candidacy because everyone believed cardinals would choose a younger man who could serve for more than a short time like Benedict.

What the Pope Believes

The 2010 book *El Jesuita* (*The Jesuit*) by Sergio Rubin and Francesca Ambrogetti is a biography of Cardinal Jorge Mario Bergoglio that is composed of conversations with the future pope. In the book, which was reprinted in 2013 as *Pope Francis: Conversations with Jorge Bergoglio*, the cardinal confessed he was getting rid of most of his books and papers because "I want to leave as little as possible behind me when I take my leave from this world." Among the papers Bergoglio said he would keep was a letter he wrote to himself shortly before he was ordained in 1969 expressing his spiritual beliefs. The letter includes the following statements, which Bergoglio said he still believed decades later:

> I believe in my history, which was infused with the loving gaze of God who, on a spring day of September 21 [1954], crossed my path and invited me to follow him.
> I believe in the kindness of others, and that I must love without fear, without ever betraying them in search of my safety.
> I believe I wish to love in abundance.
> I believe in the embracing patience of God, as gentle as a summer evening.

Sergio Rubin and Francesca Ambrogetti. *Pope Francis: Conversations with Jorge Bergoglio.* New York: G. P. Putnam's Sons, 2013, pp. 167–169.

Bergoglio was so sure he had no chance of being elected that he reserved a flight home on March 23—economy class, naturally—and had already begun to prepare for retirement. On December 17, 2011, as all bishops must on their seventy-fifth birthday, Bergoglio had submitted his resignation. Although cardinals often remain in office several years longer, Bergoglio had already chosen a retirement home where he would live with other priests. It was located in Flores, where he had grown up.

Bergoglio, however, would soon discover that God had other plans for his future.

Bergoglio Is Elected Pope

Before the papal conclave, the cardinals met to discuss issues confronting the church. Bergoglio gave a four-minute speech during those meetings. He told his fellow cardinals that the Catholic Church had become so concerned with protecting itself that it was ignoring its main mission, which was to spread the message of Jesus Christ: "When the church does not come out of herself to evangelize, she becomes self-referential and gets sick."[64]

Bergoglio's simple reminder that the church needed to be more concerned with caring for its faithful was so powerful that Havana cardinal Jaime Lucas Ortega y Alamino asked Bergoglio for a copy of his remarks. Bergoglio had spoken without notes but the next day gave his friend a written summation of his speech. Ortega y Alamino thought it was so compelling that he made it public several weeks later after a mass in Cuba, and the news media spread it around the world. Although no details of voting were released, it is believed that Bergoglio's talk swayed many cardinals to support him. Even before voting began, several cardinals told Bergoglio privately that it was his turn to head the church.

When cardinals entered the Sistine Chapel to begin voting on March 12, tens of thousands of people gathered outside to await news of a new pope. The outcome of voting at the end of each day is signaled by smoke rising from a small chimney when papal ballots are burned. The smoke is known by the Latin names *fumata nera* (black smoke) and *fumata bianca* (white smoke). Black smoke means no pope has been elected and white signifies a pope has been chosen. Chemicals are added to ballots to make sure the smoke is the right color.

At 7:05 P.M. on March 13, people erupted in shouts of joy when white smoke poured out of the chimney. On the fourth and final vote, Bergoglio received 90 of 115 votes. By tradition, Bergoglio was asked if he would accept the position. The

A nun in St. Peter's Square at the Vatican reacts to the news that a new pope has been elected in 2013.

traditional response is a simple "accepto," Latin for "I accept." Instead, Bergoglio answered, "I am a great sinner; trusting in God's mercy and patience, in suffering, I accept."[65]

The surprising response was a display of the personal humility that would help endear Francis to millions of people. His words signaled a new papal era that would continue to surprise, and often delight, the world.

A Pope Like No Other

People around the world began to realize Francis was different from past popes during his first public appearance. When Francis stepped out on the balcony overlooking St. Peter's Square at 8:33 P.M., he was clad in the white cassock, sash, and skullcap that marked his office. But television cameras and eagle-eyed observers in the crowd of more than one hundred thousand noticed Francis was not wearing the traditional fur-trimmed velvet cape. And in Buenos Aires, Father Juan Isasmendi saw another

Pope Francis waves to crowds as he arrives to his inauguration mass at the Vatican in 2013. He stunned onlookers by stopping to embrace people.

difference in attire while watching television with some of the city's poorest residents. Isasmendi noted that Francis still wore the plain metal cross he had as archbishop instead of the gold one for popes.

Because the balcony concealed his feet, no one saw that Francis still wore his old black shoes, which news stories described as battered, instead of expensive, hand-sewn red-leather loafers made exclusively for popes. When his speech was over and cardinals began filing onto a mini-bus to go back to the hotel where they had been staying, Francis joined them instead of riding in the pope's limousine. Hours later when Francis and the cardinals ate dinner, he displayed the sense of humor the world would soon know by telling them, "May God forgive you for what you've done."[66]

At 5:45 A.M. the next morning, Francis left his small room clad in the black priest clothes he had always worn instead of papal white and went to the hotel's chapel to pray as he did

Pope Francis Needs Other People

Pope Francis surprised people by choosing to live in Casa Santa Marta, a hotel that houses priests and bishops who are visiting Rome or work in Vatican City, instead of the Apostolic Palace. In an interview, Francis explained that his choice of where to live was similar to his decision to become a Jesuit because it entailed living with other priests in a communal setting:

> And then a thing that is really important for me: community. I was always looking for a community. I did not see myself as a priest on my own. I need a community. [I] chose to live here, in Room 201 [of Santa Marta], because when I took possession of the papal apartment, inside myself I distinctly heard a "no." The papal apartment in the Apostolic Palace is not luxurious. It is old, tastefully decorated and large, but not luxurious. But in the end it is like an inverted funnel. It is big and spacious, but the entrance is really tight. People can come only in dribs and drabs, and I cannot live without people. I need to live my life with others.

Antonio Spadaro. "A Big Heart Open to God." *America*, September 30, 2013. http://americamagazine.org/pope-francis-interview.

Instead of moving into the official pope's residence in the Vatican, Pope Francis chose more modest accommodations in this Casa Santa Marta apartment.

every morning. After breakfast, Francis again declined the papal limousine and was driven in a small car to the Basilica of Santa Maria Maggiore for more prayer. When security guards tried to keep people out of the church, Francis said, "I'm a pilgrim and I just want to be one among the pilgrims."[67] To protect the pope they defied that order, but when Francis left, he stopped at a schoolyard and talked to some excited children.

Francis went to the hotel in which he had stayed for two weeks before the conclave to pay his bill and collect his belongings. When a clerk waived payment, Francis paid anyway. He also asked the hotel staff to gather so he could thank them for how they had treated him. Francis then mentioned that the bulb in his bedside lamp had blown out. He asked for a bulb and went to the room, replacing the bulb and packing his own suitcase.

Later that day, Francis was shown the huge space popes had lived in since 1903 in the Apostolic Palace, which is located next to St. Peter's Basilica. Francis was overwhelmed at the size of the apartments making up the pope's living space. "There's room for three hundred people," he said. "I don't need all this space."[68] Francis decided instead to remain in Casa Santa Marta. He was given room 201, which has nicer furnishings than his room during the conclave and is larger so he can receive guests. In the next few days when Francis began signing official documents, he did it with a simple "Franciscus." He did not add the traditional but more regal *PP* suffix for *pontifix pontificum*, a Latin phrase Roman emperors once used. Pontiff, another name for pope, means "bridge builder." The *PP* suffix referred to the power emperors had to build bridges and control vast amounts of territory.

"The Carnival Is Over"

When news stories about how Francis acted during his first few days as pope spread around the world, people were amazed at his humility and rejection of many of the luxurious trappings that go with being the leader of the Catholic Church. Both made Francis instantly popular with millions of people around the

Pope Francis begins his first Sunday as pope by making an impromptu appearance to the public from a side gate of the Vatican, startling passersby and prompting cheers.

world. The demand for Francis news was so strong that reporters scrambling for details sometimes used facts they could not substantiate. One report claimed that when Francis refused to wear the fur cape after being elected, he said, "The carnival is over."[69] The quote was dramatic and many other reporters picked it up. The problem is that Francis never said it. The quote, however, accurately symbolized the start of a new papal era and summed up the new pope's intriguing personality.

Chapter 6

A Pope Full of Surprises

People were still getting to know Pope Francis when he stunned the world on March 19, 2013, with a tender gesture of love before his inaugural mass in St. Peter's Square. Francis entered the square packed with two hundred thousand admirers while standing in the back of a white jeep. As Francis drew near a group of people in wheelchairs, he hopped off the vehicle and kissed a severely disabled man cradled in the arms of another man before resuming his ride to the altar for mass.

Francis duplicated that act of love and mercy on November 6, 2013, when he embraced fifty-three-year-old Vinicio Riva, an Italian man with neurofibromatosis, a rare disease that covered his face with ugly, fleshy growths. Video and photos of Francis kissing Riva's horribly disfigured face went viral on the Internet and in news stories because of the compassion he showed toward someone most people would turn away from. Riva said the pope's hug was "like paradise," and described the encounter as: "First I kissed his hand while he, with the other hand, caressed my head and wounds. Then he drew me to him in a strong embrace, kissing my face. My head was against his chest, his arms were wrapped around me. It lasted just over a minute, but to me it seemed like an eternity."[70]

Security for the pope has been tightened ever since Pope John Paul II was shot and seriously injured in 1981 while riding in his popemobile, the nickname given to the vehicles that transport the pope. Francis's penchant for randomly jumping off the popemobile

Pope Francis kisses Vinicio Riva, an Italian man with neurofibromatosis (a condition that leads to the development of tumors) during one of his weekly papal audiences in 2013.

has become a security nightmare for his guards. However, it is these theatrics that have endeared him to millions of people by showing he is friendly, loving, and compassionate instead of aloof, authoritarian, and critical, which was the perception most people had of popes. Those dramatic actions, however, pale in importance to other things Francis does and says as he continues to defy conventional ideas about how a pope should act.

A Conservative Pope?

When Francis was elected pope, people knowledgeable about the Catholic Church expected him to be conservative like John

Paul II and Benedict because he opposed gay marriage and abortion, while supporting celibacy for priests. But Francis soon showed his liberal side by again shattering the Holy Thursday tradition that symbolizes Jesus's act of humility by washing the feet of his disciples.

On March 27, 2013, instead of washing the feet of twelve priests in church, Francis washed and kissed the feet of twelve inmates in a juvenile detention facility. Francis told the young people, "This is a symbol, it is a sign—washing your feet means I am at your service. Help one another. This is what Jesus teaches us."[71] The break with tradition was so radical that some conservative Catholics criticized Francis, especially because two of the twelve were women and two were Muslims.

The foot-washing episode was the first sign that Francis might be willing to significantly break with Catholic traditions. Four months later, Francis said something that again set him apart from previous popes. When he visited Brazil in July 2013, he drew huge, enthusiastic crowds that treated him more like a rock star than a pope. On the final day of his trip on July 28, Francis said mass to an estimated 3 million people gathered along Copacabana beach. That impressive gathering was soon overshadowed by comments Francis made to reporters as they flew home to Italy. When reporters asked Francis about gays, he

Millions of people gather in Rio de Janeiro to hear Pope Francis deliver a mass during a trip to Brazil in 2013.

told them: "If someone is gay, who searches for the Lord and has goodwill, who am I to judge? The Catechism of the Catholic Church explains this very well. It says they should not be marginalized because of this [sexual orientation] but that they must be integrated into society."[72]

The remark stunned the world. Francis had claimed he had no right to judge gays even though church officials had usually condemned them, including Benedict, who labeled homosexuality a "moral evil."[73] In an interview in the September issue of the Jesuit magazine *America*, Francis indicated he was ready to

bring that more loving attitude to other social issues that had embroiled the church in controversy.

"A Field Hospital After Battle"

For several decades, millions of Catholics had left the church because they disagreed with its opposition to abortion, gay rights, birth control, and allowing priests to marry. The church's attempt to conceal sexual misconduct by pedophile priests had also reduced the ranks of Catholics and stained its reputation with non-Catholics. A study on religion by the Pew Research Center in 2008 showed that in the United States, one in ten Americans was a former Catholic. In the *America* interview, Francis gave this blunt assessment of the Catholic Church: "I see clearly that the thing the church needs most today is the ability to heal wounds and to warm the hearts of the faithful; it needs nearness, proximity. I see the church as a field hospital after battle."[74]

The church's image has also been weakened by the public role it played in defending its increasingly unpopular stands on social issues. In the United States, some bishops and cardinals had warned Catholics not to vote for candidates that supported abortion. Francis said it was wrong for the church to center its efforts on such issues because it took time and resources away from its main job of helping people connect with God and easing problems like poverty that made their lives difficult. When American cardinal Raymond L. Burke criticized the pope by saying, "We can never talk enough about that [abortion],"[75] Francis showed he meant what he had said. Francis removed Burke from the panel that chooses bishops, which for several decades had selected only conservatives.

Instead of fighting cultural battles, Francis wanted to focus on helping people who needed help the most. In his first official trip outside Rome, Francis traveled to Lampedusa, Italy, on July 8, 2013, to spotlight the plight of people who had fled violence in North Africa. For several years tens of thousands of men, women, and children had made the dangerous voyage to this island off the coast of Italy in overcrowded boats that some-

Changing the Catholic Church

Many Catholics have left the church for decades because of policies prohibiting divorced people who remarry from receiving communion, not baptizing babies born out of wedlock, criticizing gays, and not allowing priests to marry. But Pope Francis said in a 2013 interview that "the church sometimes has locked itself up in small things, in small-minded rules."[1] His comment seemed to open the door for changes on such issues. Church policy regarding divorced people has been especially unpopular because divorce is so common. In the United States, millions of Catholics are in danger of being denied communion because 40 percent to 50 percent of marriages end in divorce. Francis has also said the church needs to do more to help divorced Catholics: "[When] this love fails—because many times it fails—we must feel the pain of the failure and accompany those who have failed in their love. Not condemn them! Walk alongside them."[2] His remarks on gays have made people believe that Francis's more loving and flexible attitude has made them more welcome in church. And although Francis supports celibacy for priests, he has said it is a rule that could be changed.

1. Antonio Spadaro. "A Big Heart Open to God." *America*, September 30, 2013. http://americamagazine.org/pope-francis-interview.

2. Cindy Wood. "Pope Urges Sympathy, Outreach to Couples Whose Marriages Fail." Catholic News Service, February 28, 2014. http://ncronline.org/blogs/francis-chronicles/pope-urges-sympathy-outreach-couples-whose-marriages-fail.

times sank, killing hundreds of people. Thousands of them still lived in harsh conditions in refugee camps on Lampedusa while officials decided what to do with them.

During mass on the shore of the Mediterranean Sea, Francis, the son of immigrants, said the world was wrong not to help them: "We have become used to other people's suffering, it

During his first trip as pope, Francis greets African immigrants on the Italian island of Lampedusa in July 2013.

doesn't concern us, it doesn't interest us, it's none of our business!"[76] The pope later tweeted, "We pray for a heart which will embrace immigrants. God will judge us upon how we have treated the most needy."[77]

Francis showed that same concern for the poor in criticizing the global economy in *Evangelii Gaudium* (*Joy of the Gospel*), a 224-page document he wrote. Released in November 2013, it explores ways Catholics can use the Bible to deepen their faith and share it with other people. But in a section on challenges facing the world, Francis claimed that today's capitalist economy enables a small group of people to become wealthy while dooming many more to poverty: "[We] have to say 'thou shalt not' to an economy of exclusion and inequality. Such an economy kills. . . . While the earnings of a minority are growing exponentially, so too is the gap separating the majority from the prosperity enjoyed by those happy few."[78]

Many economists and political leaders, including U.S. president Barack Obama, have warned that global income inequality is a growing problem. When Francis delivered the same mes-

"This Is the Pope Calling."

Pope Francis called Buenos Aires, Argentina, the day after he was elected to cancel his newspaper subscription. It was the first of many surprise calls Francis made to people around the world to earn the nickname "the Cold Call Pope." Francis called an Italian woman who refused her boyfriend's request to have an abortion and said he would baptize the baby when it was born. He called to console a woman in Argentina who had been raped by a police officer. One call that received global attention was to wish Happy New Year to Carmelite nuns in Spain. When no one answered, the pope left a voice mail in which he jokingly asked, "What are the nuns doing that they can't answer? I am Pope Francis, I wish to greet you in this end of the year, I will see if I can call you later. May God bless you!" The nuns had been busy praying. They were mortified they missed the call, but Francis called back later. The nuns helped spread his phone message globally by giving it to a Catholic radio station. Tweets and handwritten letters have also made Francis the most accessible pope ever for average people.

Radina Gigova and Al Goodman. "Pope Francis Leaves New Year's Voice Mail for Nuns in Spain." CNN World, January 4, 2014. www.cnn.com/2014/01/04/world/europe /spain-pope-nuns-message.

sage, his words carried more moral weight. As a result, people who support a capitalist economy, even if it produces income inequality, attacked him; some even claimed his statements expressed Communist philosophy. James Martin, a Jesuit priest and political commentator, was one of many people who defended Francis. Martin said the pope's comments reflected Catholic social teaching and was based on Jesus Christ's teaching that "[we must] care for the 'least' of our brothers and sisters."[79] Martin said that an economy that allows only a minority of people to become wealthy at the expense of others violated Christian beliefs.

The pope's bold statements should not have surprised anyone because Francis had made similar remarks in the past. And no one should have been surprised at his austere lifestyle or concern for the poor because Francis had acted that way as bishop and archbishop. People also should not have been surprised, though millions were, at the way Francis worked to improve the Catholic Church's relations with other faiths.

The Pope As Peacemaker

Pentecostalism is a movement within Protestantism that emphasizes the need for a personal relationship with God. Pentecostal religious services are lively and emotional. The Catholic Church's relations with Pentecostals have been cool, partly because many Catholics joined Pentecostal churches. But in March 2014, Francis recorded an eight-minute iPhone video in which he told Pentecostals that a shared belief in Christianity is more important than any differences between them: "Come on, we are brothers. Let's give each other a spiritual hug and let God complete the work that he has begun."[80] The video went viral on emails to Pentecostals and the Internet and opened a new bond between Catholics and Pentecostals.

Francis also strengthened interfaith relations during his three-day Middle East visit in May 2014 when he became the first pope to travel there with Jewish and Muslim leaders. Rabbi Abraham Skorka and Sheikh Omar Abboud, good friends of Francis from Argentina, accompanied Francis to an area that is holy to all three religions. Francis also dared to insert himself into the troubled relationship between Israeli Jews and Palestinian Muslims, who have fought for decades over land they both claim.

The pope stopped and prayed at the Wall of Bethlehem, which is part of a massive line of walls separating Israelis from Palestinians in the disputed territory. The pope leaned his head against the wall covered with graffiti that read "Free Palestine" and prayed for several minutes. The Catholic Church for decades has recommended that both sides should compromise to

Pope Francis prays at a wall that separates Israelis from Palestinians in disputed West Bank territory during a visit to the Middle East in 2014.

settle the dispute; instead, Israelis and Palestinians have continued to hate and sometimes use violence against each other as they have failed to settle their differences. During mass in Bethlehem on May 25, Francis made an extraordinary offer to Israeli President Shimon Peres and Palestine Authority President Mahmoud Abbas by inviting them to meet with him in Rome on June 8 in a prayer summit. Peace talks between the leaders brokered by the United States had broken down a month earlier and Francis wanted the leaders to meet in a neutral place to see if they could agree to more talks.

On June 8, 2014, Peres and Abbas met with Francis in a garden behind St. Peter's Basilica. The meeting featured Christian, Jewish, and Muslim prayers, and the three planted an olive tree as a symbol of peace. In brief remarks before the ceremony, Francis said.

> It is my hope that this meeting will mark the beginning of a new journey where we seek things that unite, so as to overcome the things that divide. Peacemaking calls for courage, much more so than warfare. It calls for the courage to say yes to encounter and no to conflict, yes to dialogue and no to violence. [81]

Although the effort failed to restart talks, the fact that both leaders agreed to meet in Rome was a testament to how powerful and influential Francis had become in little more than a year as pope. In fact, some people even considered Francis a superhero.

Super Pope?

In January 2014, Maupal, a Rome graffiti artist, drew a picture of Pope Francis on a wall near St. Peter's Square in which Francis, clad in a white cape, is soaring into the air like Superman. The source of his powers was evident in the briefcase he clutched in one hand that read *valores*, Italian for "values." Many people who admired Francis claimed the image dubbed "Super Pope" was an appropriate tribute. Rome resident Daniela Di LucaBossa said, "I think he is a true super hero, because he has changed people's hearts because he is really showing us all how to live. So in this light, there isn't a better representation for him."[82] Francis, however, rejected the comparison: "Depicting the pope to be a sort of superman, a type of star, seems offensive to me. The pope is a man who laughs, cries, sleeps calmly and has friends like everyone—a normal person."[83]

The world, however, has considered Francis someone very special ever since he became pope. His smiling face was on the cover of *Time* in December 2013 when the magazine named him its Person of the Year. Managing editor Nancy Gibbs wrote that Francis has rapidly become one of the world's most influential and famous people because of the extraordinary love he shows

A street art mural by Maupal depicting Pope Francis as a super hero is popular with many. Pope Francis, though, finds it offensive as he is just a "normal person."

for everyone in what he does and says: "When he kisses the face of a disfigured man or washes the feet of a Muslim woman, the image resonates far beyond the boundaries of the Catholic Church."[84]

Francis also made the February 13, 2014 cover of *Rolling Stone*, a magazine usually devoted to rock stars, and he was lavishly praised again a month later in publications around the world on the anniversary of his election. Mark Binelli, who has written extensively about Francis, claimed the world loves him because "his recognizable humanity comes across as positively revolutionary."[85] Cardinal Seán P. O'Malley of Boston, a

Two Popes

When Pope Francis was elected, many people speculated his reign would be complicated because Pope Benedict XVI was still alive. Instead the two popes have had an easy, cordial relationship because Francis likes Benedict. Argentine journalist Jorge Milia, once a student of the pope, said Francis told him he enjoys talking to Benedict, whom he calls "el viejo," the affectionate Spanish term for "old man." But Milia said Francis also considers Benedict a source of wisdom and knowledge: "It's a pleasure for me to exchange ideas with him. [You] can't imagine the humility and wisdom of this man. I wouldn't even consider giving up the counsel of a person like this, it would be foolish on my part!" Another reason for their friendly relationship is that Benedict is content with retirement and has not tried to publicly upstage Francis. And Francis has honored Benedict by including him in important public events. Francis invited Benedict to the April 27, 2014 ceremony in which he officially declared Popes John XXIII and John Paul II saints. The news media billed the event as "the day of the four popes" because Benedict was there to share the day honoring the two new saints.

Andrea Tornielli. "'It Would Be Foolish to Turn Down Benedict's Advice,'" Francis Tells Former Pupil." *La Stampa*, July 11, 2013. http://vaticaninsider.lastampa.it/en/the-vatican /detail/articolo/papa-pope-el-papa-riforma-reform-reforma-26403.

Franciscan who led a panel discussion of other cardinals on Francis, said, "The pope is a true companion of Jesus."[86] Lino Cattaruzzi, president of Google Argentina, said what Francis has done has made him great: "What matters most is that we can see Papa Francisco has the right core values, that he makes good judgments on questions like wealth distribution, that he is humble and simple, and that he lives as he speaks."[87]

Some of his critics, however, claim that even though Francis has become a beloved and respected global figure, his words and deeds are largely symbolic. They argue that he has not changed Catholic policies many people disagree with or brought many former Catholics back to the church. But more people believe that Francis has achieved a great deal in a very short time as pope.

"It's Like a Healing Balm"

Although there has been no dramatic increase in attendance, Francis has inspired some Catholics, including Cattaruzzi, to attend mass again regularly. Crowds at his weekly appearances in St. Peter's Square have tripled in size. Father Enrico Feroci, who heads the Catholic charity Caritas in Rome, said the pope's concern for the poor has dramatically increased the number of volunteers for its meal and homeless programs. Polls in several countries have shown that Catholics overwhelmingly admire Francis and that he has given them a renewed strength in their faith. John Unni, pastor of St. Cecilia Parish in Boston, said because of Francis "there's an energy, a feeling, a spirit here. It's like a healing balm."[88]

Cardinal O'Malley agrees that Francis has dramatically changed how people feel about the church itself. O'Malley said, "I like the phrase that someone said, that he is not changing the lyrics but only the melody."[89] And Father James Martin, a respected commentator in the media about Catholicism, claims changing the tone of the church's message has already accomplished a lot:

> Frankly, a change in tone is a real change. You look at the number of people who feel more welcome today in the church. And you can include among those gays and lesbians, women, divorced and remarried Catholics, people who struggle with various church teachings. They all tell me that they feel more welcome, and that's a change.[90]

Francis has thus been able to change attitudes and perceptions many people hold about the Catholic Church. Guillermo Marcó, Bergoglio's media spokesman for eight years, says the reason that Francis has been able to do that is simple: "It is the first time we have had a priest as Pope."[91] By that, Marcó means that Francis still cares about helping individual people as much as any parish priest. Many popes had spent so many years as administrators or academics that they had lost the common touch average priests have in dealing with people. But even as a cardinal, Francis mingled daily with average people including some of the poorest on earth. Francis has never lost that human, caring quality, the need he expresses in loving and sincerely wanting to help people, that has made him so popular and has been the key to his success.

Introduction: The Surprise Pope

1. Quoted in Joshua J. McElwee. "Cardinals Elect Pope Francis, Argentinean Jesuit Jorge Mario Bergoglio." *National Catholic Reporter*, March 13, 2013. http://ncronline.org /news/vatican/cardinals-elect-pope-francis-argentinean -jesuit-jorge-mario-bergoglio.
2. Quoted in Jim Yardley. "A Surprise Choice from Afar, Winning Over Some Skeptics." *New York Times*, March 13, 2013. www.nytimes.com/2013/03/14/world/europe/rome -meets-surprise-pick-in-the-square.html?_r=0.
3. Quoted in Michael Collins. *Francis, Bishop of Rome*. Collegeville, MN: Liturgical, 2013, p. 97.
4. Quoted in Pope Francis. "@Pontifex, The Official Twitter Page of His Holiness Pope Francis." March 13, 2013. https://twitter.com/Pontifex.
5. Quoted in Nick Squires. "Pope Francis Says He Chose His Name Because He Wants a 'Church of the Poor, for the Poor.'" *Telegraph* (London), March 16, 2013. www.tele graph.co.uk/news/religion/the-pope/9934596/Pope -Francis-says-he-chose-his-name-because-he-wants-a -Church-of-the-poor-for-the-poor.html.

Chapter 1: A Humble Beginning

6. Quoted in "'Jorge Is Against Regimes. It Is Because of Fascism That Our Father Emigrated.'" *Vatican Insider*, March 17, 2013. www.lastampa.it/2013/03/17/esteri /vatican-insider/en/translate-to-english-jorge-e-contro -i-regimi-colpa-del-fascismo-se-nostro-padre-emigro -dsLa2d3qBmg6w2j0djj5qK/pagina.html.
7. Quoted in Andrea Tornielli. *Francis: Pope of a New World*. San Francisco, CA: Ignatius, 2013, p. 75.
8. Quoted in Collins. *Francis, Bishop of Rome*, p. 13.
9. Quoted in Silvina Frydlewsky and Anthony Faiola. "Bergoglio Challenged Moral Authority of Argentina's Elected

Leaders." *Washington Post*, March 14, 2013. www
.washingtonpost.com/world/the_americas/bergoglio
-challenged-moral-authority-of-argentinas-elected
-leaders/2013/03/14/95db94f6-8ce7-11e2-b63f-f53fb
9f2fcb4_story.html.

10. Quoted in Mario Escobar. *Francis: Man of Prayer*. Nash-
    ville, TN: Thomas Nelson, 2013, p. 7.
11. Quoted in Sergio Rubin and Francesca Ambrogetti.
    Pope Francis: Conversations with Jorge Bergoglio. New York:
    G. P. Putnam's Sons, 2013, p. 15.
12. Quoted in Nick Squires. "Pope Francis: 'He Always
    Cooked Fantastic Paella.'" *Telegraph* (London), Novem-
    ber 18, 2013. www.telegraph.co.uk/news/religion/the
    -pope/10457468/Pope-Francis-He-always-cooked-fantastic
    -paella.html.
13. Quoted in Paulo Prada and Helen Popper. "Special
    Report: Behind the Charm, a Political Pope." Reuters,
    March 27, 2013. www.reuters.com/article/2013/03/27/us
    -pope-profile-specialreport-idUSBRE92Q09P20130327.
14. Jorge Mario Bergoglio. "The Story of a Vocation."
    L'Osservatore Romano, January 3, 2014. http://vatican
    resources.s3.amazonaws.com/pdf%2FING_2014_001
    _0301.pdf.
15. Quoted in Rubin and Ambrogetti. *Pope Francis*, p. 34.
16. Quoted in Tornielli. *Francis: Pope of a New World*, p. 82.
17. Quoted in Father Roger Landry. "The 60th Anniversary
    of Pope Francis' Calling: How the Feast of St. Matthew
    Changed the Holy Father's Life." *National Catholic Register*,
    September 21, 2013. www.ncregister.com/site/article/the
    -60th-anniversary-of-pope-francis-calling.

Chapter 2: A Jesuit

18. Quoted in Rubin and Ambrogetti. *Pope Francis*, p. 39.
19. Quoted in Peter Stanford. "Pope Francis Anniversary:
    'I've Done Things Well. I've Done Things Wrong.'" *Tele-
    graph* (London), March 7, 2014. www.telegraph.co.uk
    /news/religion/the-pope/10678510/Pope-Francis-anniver
    sary-Ive-done-things-well.-Ive-done-things-wrong.html.

20. Quoted in Thomas J. Craughwell. *Pope Francis: The Pope from the End of the Earth*. Charlotte, NC: Saint Benedict, 2013, p. 85.

21. Bergoglio. "The Story of a Vocation."

22. Quoted in Tornielli. *Francis: Pope of a New World*, p. 85.

23. Antonio Spadaro. "A Big Heart Open to God." *America*, September 30, 2013. http://americamagazine.org/pope -francis-interview.

24. Quoted in Rubin and Ambrogetti. *Pope Francis*, p. 38.

25. Quoted in Carolina Contreras. "Pope Francis Studied in Chile." InfoSurHoy.com, April 4, 2013. http://infosurhoy .com/en_GB/articles/saii/features/society/2013/04/04 /feature-01?source=related.

26. Quoted in Carol Glatz. "Former Student Recalls Life Lessons from Literature Teacher, the Pope." Catholic News Service, March 12, 2014. www.catholicnews.com/data /stories/cns/1401032.htm.

27. Quoted in Rubin and Ambrogetti. *Pope Francis*, p. 51.

28. Quoted in Jorge Milia. "Bergoglio and Borges: Truths and Tales of a 'Friendship.'" *Vatican Insider*, December 6, 2013. http://vaticaninsider.lastampa.it/en/world-news /detail/articolo/borges-borges-borges-francesco-francis -francisco-30459.

29. Quoted in Rubin and Ambrogetti. *Pope Francis*, p. 53.

30. Jorge Mario Bergoglio and Abraham Skorka. *On Heaven and Earth: Pope Francis on Faith, Family and the Church in the Twenty-First Century*. New York: Image, 2013, p. 47.

31. Quoted in Paul Vallely. *Pope Francis: Untying the Knots*. London: Bloomsbury, 2013, p. 32.

Chapter 3: Bishop Bergoglio

32. Quoted in James Martin. "Jesuit Formation." *John Carroll Magazine*, November 12, 2013. http://sites.jcu.edu /magazine/2013/11/12/jesuit-formation.

33. Quoted in Collins. *Francis, Bishop of Rome*, p. 32.

34. Quoted in Spadaro. "A Big Heart Open to God."

35. Quoted in Rubin and Ambrogetti. *Pope Francis*, p. 213.

36. Iain Guest. *Behind the Disappearances: Argentina's Dirty War Against Human Rights and the United Nations*. Philadelphia, PA: University of Pennsylvania Press, 1990, p. 36.
37. Quoted in Uki Goñi. "The New Pope and Argentina's 'Disappeared' of the Dirty War." *Time*, March 14, 2013. http://world.time.com/2013/03/14/the-new-pope-and-argentinas-disappeared-of-the-dirty-war.
38. Quoted in Spadaro. "A Big Heart Open to God."
39. Quoted in Stanford. "Pope Francis Anniversary."
40. Quoted in Rubin and Ambrogetti. *Pope Francis*, p. 46.
41. Quoted in Vallely. *Pope Francis: Untying the Knots*, p. 128.
42. Quoted in Collins. *Francis, Bishop of Rome*, p. 37.
43. Quoted in Spadaro. "A Big Heart Open to God."
44. Quoted in Haley Cohen. "Slum Priests: Pope Francis's Early Years." *Atlantic*, March 20, 2013. www.theatlantic.com/international/archive/2013/03/slum-priests-pope-franciss-early-years/274201.

Chapter 4: Cardinal Bergoglio

45. Quoted in Rubin and Ambrogetti. *Pope Francis*, p. xxiv.
46. Quoted in Squires. "Pope Francis: "He Always Cooked Fantastic Paella."
47. Quoted in Collins. Francis, Bishop of Rome, p. 47.
48. Quoted in Tom Hennigan, "Argentina Legalises Gay Marriage." *Irish Times*, July 16, 2010, p. 18.
49. Quoted in Rafael Romo, Jose Manuel Rodriguez and Catherine E. Shoichet. "Behind Closed Doors, Pope Supported Civil Unions in Argentina, Activist Says." CNN World, March 21, 2013. www.cnn.com/2013/03/20/world/americas/argentina-pope-civil-unions.
50. Quoted in Tornielli. *Francis: Pope of a New World*, p. 118.
51. Quoted in Vallely. *Pope Francis: Untying the Knots*, p. 130.
52. Quoted in Gianni Valente. "We Are Not Owners of the Gifts of the Lord." 30Giorni, August 2009. www.30giorni.it/articoli_id_21539_l3.htm.

53. Quoted in Rubin and Ambrogetti. *Pope Francis*, p. 129.
54. Quoted in Silvina Frydlewsky and Anthony Faiola. "Bergoglio Tested by Argentine Leaders." *Washington Post*, March 14, 2013. www.washingtonpost.com/world /the_americas/bergoglio-challenged-moral-authority-of -argentinas-elected-leaders/2013/03/14/95db94f6-8ce7 -11e2-b63f-f53fb9f2fcb4_story.html.
55. Quoted in Tornielli. *Francis: Pope of a New World*, p. 128.
56. Quoted in Vallely. *Pope Francis: Untying the Knots*, p. 116.
57. Quoted in John L. Allen Jr. "Profile: New Pope, Jesuit Bergoglio, Was Runner-Up in 2005 Conclave." *National Catholic Reporter*, March 3, 2013. http://ncronline .org/blogs/ncr-today/papabile-day-men-who-could-be -pope-13.
58. Quoted in Francis Chamberlain. "Good News from Brazil." *America*, August 27, 2007. http://americamaga zine.org/issue/623/article/good-news-brazil.

Chapter 5: Bergoglio Becomes Pope Francis

59. Quoted in Leslie Scrivener. "Ordinary People Love Him." *Toronto Star*, April 5, 2005, p. A6.
60. Quoted in Nicole Windfield. "Cardinal Diary Details Papal Conclave." *USA Today*, September 24, 2005. http:// usatoday30.usatoday.com/news/religion/2005-09-23-papal -conclave_x.htm.
61. Quoted in Rubin and Ambrogetti. *Pope Francis*, p. 164.
62. Quoted in "Pope Renounces Papal Throne." Vatican Information Service, February 11, 2013. http://visnews -en.blogspot.ca/2013/02/pope-renounces-papal-throne .html.
63. Allen. "Profile: New Pope, Jesuit Bergoglio."
64. Quoted in Sandro Magister. "The Last Words of Ber- goglio Before the Conclave." *Chiesa Espresso*, March 27, 2013. http://chiesa.espresso.repubblica.it/articolo/135 0484?eng=y.
65. Quoted in Collins. *Francis, Bishop of Rome*, p. 93.

66. Quoted in Mark Binelli. "Francis: The People's Pope." *Independent* [Dublin], March 2, 2014. www.independent .ie/lifestyle/francis-the-peoples-pope-30044999.html.

67. Quoted in Craughwell. *Pope Francis: The Pope from the End of the Earth*, p. 36.

68. Quoted in Vallely. *Pope Francis: Untying the Knots*, p. 173.

69. Quoted in John L. Allen Jr. "Debunking Three 'Urban Legends' about Pope Francis." *National Catholic Reporter*, March 24, 2013. http://ncronline.org/blogs/ncr-today /debunking-three-urban-legends-about-pope-francis.

Chapter 6: A Pope Full of Surprises

70. Quoted in Hannah Roberts. "'It Was Like Being in Paradise. I Felt Only Love': Terribly Disfigured Man Who Was Held by the Pope Relives the Moment That Moved the World." *Daily Mail* [London], November 18, 2013. www .dailymail.co.uk/news/article-2509528/Vinicio-Riva -disfigured-man-met-Pope.html.

71. Quoted in Nicole Winfield. "Pope Francis Washes Feet of Young Detainees in Ritual." *USA Today*, March 28, 2013. www.usatoday.com/story/news/world/2013/03/28 /pope-frances-washes-feet/2028595.

72. Quoted in Anne Thompson and Henry Austin. "Pope: 'Who Am I to Judge?' Gay People." NBC News, July 29, 2013. www.nbcnews.com/news/other/pope-who-am-i -judge-gay-people-f6C10780741.

73. Quoted in Binelli. "Francis: The People's Pope."

74. Quoted in Spadaro. "A Big Heart Open to God."

75. Quoted in Jim Yardley and Jason Horowitz. "Pope Replaces Conservative U.S. Cardinal on Influential Vatican Committee." *New York Times*, December 16, 2013. www .nytimes.com/2013/12/17/world/europe/pope-replaces -conservative-us-cardinal-on-influential-vatican-committee .html.

76. Quoted in Peter Finocchiaro. "Pope Francis Sounds Pro-Immigrant Message in Lampedusa During First Official Trip Outside Rome." *Huffington Post*, July 8, 2013.

www.huffingtonpost.com/2013/07/08/pope-francis
-immigration_n_3560803.html.

77. Quoted in Pope Francis. "@Pontifex, the Official Twitter Page of His Holiness Pope Francis." July 8, 2013. https://twitter.com/Pontifex.

78. Quoted in Pope Francis. *Apostolic Exhortation of the Holy Father Francis: The Joy of the Gospel (Evangelii Gaudium).* http://w2.vatican.va/content/francesco/en/apost _exhortations/documents/papa-francesco_esortazione -ap_20131124_evangelii-gaudium.html.

79. Quoted in Annysa Johnson. "Catholic Church Is a Big Tent, 'Colbert' Chaplain James Martin says." *Milwaukee Journal Sentinel,* May 13, 2014. www.jsonline.com/news /religion/catholic-church-is-a-big-tent-colbert-chaplain -james-martin-says-b99268396z1-259159301.html#axzz 31obLPddU.

80. Quoted in Rachel Zoll. "Pope Francis Sparks New Era in Catholic-Pentecostal Ties with Unusual Message and Messengers." *New Europe Online,* March 28, 2013. www .neurope.eu/news/wire/pope-francis-sparks-new-era -catholic-pentecostal-ties-unusual-message-messengers.

81. Quoted in Josephine McKenna and Inna Lazareva. "Pope Francis Calls for Israelis and Palestinians to 'Break Spiral of Violence.'" *The Telegraph* [London], June 8, 2014. www.telegraph.co.uk/news/worldnews/the -pope/10885417/Pope-Francis-calls-for-Israelis-and -Palestinians-to-break-spiral-of-violence.html.

82. Quoted in Sharon Reich, "Move Over Superman: It's Time for 'Superpope.'" Reuters, January 29, 2014. http:// uk.reuters.com/video/2014/01/29/move-over-superman- its-time-for-superpop?videoId=276639902.

83. Quoted in Amy Davidson. "Francis and the Superman Problem." *New Yorker,* March 6, 2014. www.newyorker .com/online/blogs/closeread/2014/03/pope-francis-and -the-superman-problem.html.

84. Quoted in Nancy Gibbs. "Pope Francis, the Choice." *Time,* December 22, 2013. http://poy.time.com/2013 /12/11/pope-francis-the-choice.

85. Binelli. "Francis: The People's Pope."

86. Quoted in Maria Wiering. "Cardinal, Panelists: Pope Francis' Celebrity Should Turn Eyes to Jesus." *Catholic News Service*, March 20, 2014. http://ncronline.org/news /faith-parish/cardinal-panelists-pope-francis-celebrity -should-turn-eyes-jesus.

87. Quoted in Stanford. "Pope Francis Anniversary."

88. Quoted in Daniel Burke. "How to Really Measure the 'Francis Effect.'" CNN, March 13, 2014. www.cnn.com /2014/03/08/living/pope-francis-effect-boston/index.html.

89. Quoted in Antonio M. Enrique. "Cardinal Reflects on Pope Francis' First Year." *Boston Pilot*, March 7, 2014. www.pilotcatholicnews.com/m/article.asp?id=17075.

90. Quoted in Johnson. "Catholic Church Is a Big Tent."

91. Quoted in Howard Chua-Eoan and Elizabeth Dias. "Pope Francis, The People's Pope." *Time*, December 11, 2013. http://poy.time.com/2013/12/11/person-of-the-year -pope-francis-the-peoples-pope.

1936
December 17, Jorge Mario Bergoglio is born in Buenos Aires, Argentina.

1954
September 21, an experience in church makes Bergoglio realize he wants to be a priest.

1956
Bergoglio begins his studies to become a priest.

1957
Bergoglio becomes gravely ill with severe pneumonia, necessitating partial removal of his right lung in August.

1958
March 11, Bergoglio joins the Society of Jesus.

1964–1965
Bergoglio teaches at a Jesuit secondary school in Santa Fe, Argentina.

1969
December 13, Bergoglio is ordained a priest.

1973–1979
Bergoglio heads the Jesuit Province that includes Argentina and Uruguay.

1979–1986
Bergoglio is rector of Colegio Máximo, a seminary near Buenos Aires.

1986–1990
Bergoglio teaches at Colegio Máximo and Colegio del Salvador.

1990
Bergoglio is moved to the Jesuit community in Córdoba, Argentina, because he is not getting along with Jesuits in Buenos Aires.

1992
May 20, Bergoglio is named an auxiliary bishop of Buenos Aires.

1998
February 28, Bergoglio becomes archbishop of Buenos Aires.

2001
February 21, Bergoglio becomes a cardinal.

2005
April 19, Bergoglio finishes second in the voting to German Cardinal Joseph Ratzinger, who becomes Pope Benedict XVI.

2013
March 13, Bergoglio is elected pope.
March 27, Pope Francis breaks tradition on Holy Thursday by washing the feet of twelve juvenile offenders.
November, *Evangelii Gaudium* (*Joy of the Gospel*), a book-length document by Pope Francis, is published.

2014
May 24–26, Pope Francis makes a pilgrimage to the Holy Land, visiting Jordan, Israel, and Palestine.

Books

Jorge Mario Bergoglio and Abraham Skorka. *On Heaven and Earth: Pope Francis on Faith, Family and the Church in the Twenty-First Century*. New York: Image, 2013. Cardinal Bergoglio and Skorka, a Jewish rabbi, discuss various religious, social, and cultural topics from the perspectives of their religions.

Michael Collins. *Francis, Bishop of Rome*. Collegeville, MN: Liturgical, 2013. Collins, a Roman Catholic priest who also profiled Pope Benedict XVI, has written a solid biography of Francis.

Mario Escobar. *Francis: Man of Prayer*. Dallas, TX: Thomas Nelson, 2013. Escobar traces Bergoglio's life from childhood to his election as pope.

Pope Francis. *Evangelii Gaudium (Joy of the Gospel): Apostolic Exhortation of the Holy Father Francis*. Rome: The Vatican, 2013. http://w2.vatican.va/content/francesco/en/apost_exhorta tions/documents/papa-francesco_esortazione-ap_20131124 _evangelii-gaudium.html. In a downloadable e-book, the pope provides his vision for the role of the gospel in today's world in a exhortation addressed to bishops, the clergy, consecrated persons, and faithful lay people.

Sergio Rubin and Francesca Ambrogetti. *Pope Francis: Conversations with Jorge Bergoglio*. New York: G. P. Putnam's Sons, 2013. This book, first published in 2010, is based on wide-ranging interviews with then-Cardinal Bergoglio and includes many interesting details about the pope's life.

Andrea Tornielli. *Francis: Pope of a New World*. San Francisco, CA: Ignatius, 2013. This veteran Italian journalist provides key insights into how and why Francis has conducted his papacy like no other pope before him.

Paul Vallely. *Pope Francis: Untying the Knots*. London: Bloomsbury, 2013. This biography closely examines the pope's life, including an in-depth discussion of the controversy concerning his involvement in Argentina's Dirty War.

Internet Sites

The First Anniversary of Pope Francis' Pontificate (www .vatican.va/auguri-francesco/pont_2014/en/index.html). Visitors to this website may browse a downloadable e-book of photographs and quotations of Francis's first year as pope.

The Guardian: **Pope Francis** (www.theguardian.com/world /pope-francis). This portal for the London, England, newspaper *The Guardian* compiles the website's stories, pictures, and videos about Pope Francis.

Huff Post: Pope Francis (www.huffingtonpost.com/news /pope-francis). This *Huffington Post* portal includes links to the media site's stories, pictures, and videos about Pope Francis.

Twitter: @Pontifex (https://twitter.com/Pontifex). The pope's official Twitter page gives its more than 4 million followers access to posts by His Holiness and other links of interest.

The Vatican: Francis (www.vatican.va/holy_father/francesco /index.htm). The Catholic Church's official site for the pope has photographs, a biography, speeches, homilies, prayers, and other material on Pope Francis.

Vatican Insider (http://vaticaninsider.lastampa.it/en). The English-language version of this website, which is part of the Italian newspaper *La Stampa*, is an excellent source of news about Pope Francis.

About the Author

Michael V. Uschan has written ninety-five books including *Life of an American Soldier in Iraq*, for which he won the 2005 Council for Wisconsin Writers Juvenile Nonfiction Award. It was the second time he won the award. Mr. Uschan began his career as a writer and editor with United Press International, a wire service that provides stories to newspapers, radio, and television. Journalism is sometimes called "history in a hurry." Mr. Uschan considers writing history books a natural extension of the skills he developed in his many years as a journalist. He and his wife, Barbara, reside in the Milwaukee suburb of Franklin, Wisconsin.